"Congratulations,
Welcome to Alaska."

Doug Drinkhaus

WILD ALASKA

by Doug Lindstrand

Wildlife Treasury

DEDICATION

Today, as we enter a new millennium, wildlife seems to be flourishing and is reestablishing itself into former ranges either naturally or through transplantation. The trend certainly seems positive and praise must be given to those whose vision and hard work have contributed to the welfare of these wild creatures. Whether they are government employees who often risk their lives enforcing laws or whether they are retired citizens who have devoted their time and energy to conservation efforts, all must be congratulated. This portfolio of Alaskan wildlife is dedicated to these often under-appreciated people.

Bald eagles

Grizzly

Author's Journal *(June 20, '81)*

To become a wildlife artist there is no place to go but to nature itself. Only there can one find the answer to what it is he seeks. No books or lectures can teach a young artist like the teachings to be found at nature's hand and in her wild realm.

WILD ALASKA

©2002 Douglas W. Lindstrand
LC Control Number: 2001 133109
ISBN: 1-928722-01-6

Publisher: Sourdough Studio
Computer Layout: Mary Humphrey
Printed in Korea
Printing and binding through
AIPEX, Inc. Seattle

First U.S. Edition: April, 2002

✸✸ Book Orders ✸✸ : Please contact your favorite bookstore.

or: Sourdough Studio
        P.O. Box 92205
        Anchorage, Alaska 99509   www.sourdoughstudio.com

<u>Other books by author</u>

"ALASKA SKETCHBOOK" ISBN 1-56523-142-2
"DRAWING BIG GAME" ISBN 1-56523-140-6
"DRAWING MAMMALS" ISBN 1-56523-141-4
"DRAWING AMERICA'S WILDLIFE" ISBN 0-9608290-6-7

All photographs by author except:
Calvin Hall: Pages 10 (B), 35
Vic Van Ballenberghe: Pages 26 (L), 146, 147, 149 (T), 181
Ole Westby : Pages 129 (T), 130

Because the primary purpose of this book was to portray the animals to the viewer, I chose to use a few "better" photographs that were taken outside Alaska's borders.

CONTENTS

A Great Horned owl fluffs up its feathers following a brief summer shower. The "horned" owl is found scattered across much of Alaska and is one of the largest of owls, with a wing span of over 4 feet. Its "hoo, hoo-hoo, hoo" is a very familiar wildlife sound.

It's springtime and a Sitka blacktail fawn scampers around his new world. During the next formative months he will rely upon his mother for food, safety and education.

AUTHOR'S INTRODUCTION

Alaska is truly a wild land. Alaska is a land of few roads and people, but a land blessed with vast tracts of wilderness and unique wildlife. Unspoiled and untamed, it is often referred to as the "Last Frontier" and "Land of the Midnight Sun". Natural beauty, bountiful resources and friendly people help insure its place amongst America's treasures.

Today, more and more people are choosing to see Alaska. Perhaps it is the 49th-state's somewhat frontier atmosphere, perhaps its grand vistas or great fishing, or, most likely, the abundant wildlife. Wild animals, after all, have always held a special place in people's hearts. To watch these beautiful creatures running free across unspoiled terrain is a sight to behold. Who could not smile while watching a band of caribou trot across autumn-colored tundra, or while watching a newborn Dall lamb play in a mountain meadow.

Alaska is also a place that draws certain residents. To live here is not for everyone. Although Alaska has a thriving economy and industrious residents, it also harbors a large percentage of outdoor-oriented people that live here merely because it is different than the "outside" world. For the most part, Alaska still lacks the crowds, hustle, and limitations that much of America now experiences. Many of those that call Alaska "home" are individuals that enjoy a more simple and less hectic lifestyle. For this reason and because of the wildlife, Alaska has become my chosen "home".

During my "Alaska years" from 1970 to the present, I have tried (and hope to continue) to keep recording and enjoying this great and wondrous North Country. I have studied, painted, and filmed its magnificent wildlife, prospected for its elusive gold, mushed teams of dogs across its unspoiled landscapes, battled king-sized King salmon in its wild rivers, flown ultralight aircraft across its frozen lakes, wintered alone at remote cabins, and more and more fell in love with this Grand Lady called Alaska. In my own small way, I want to be a part of this State's grand adventure.

This book, "Wild Alaska", is a synopsis of photos and sketches taken over a thirty-year free-lance career as I traveled about Alaska. The photographs will identify the animal and the sketches, maps, and text will give the reader a biological description as well as reference to its environment and behavior. Hopefully it will bring a greater understanding and appreciation of these magnificent and unique wildlife creatures of Alaska. May they be our treasured neighbors for countless generations.

Doug Lindstrand

laska

is a land of spectacular scenery and contrasting vistas.

"....no other part of the earth known to man
surpasses Alaska in imposing and beautiful
scenery"

John Muir

   A July scene from Denali National Park. The pink blooms of the fireweed contrast with the white slopes of Mount McKinley. At over 20,300 feet, it is the tallest mountain in North America.
   Mount McKinley is often referred to as "Denali", a word that is derived from the Athabaskan word "Deenaalee".

Located between Cook Inlet and the Chugach Mountains, Anchorage is Alaska's largest city. It is as far west as Honolulu, Hawaii and as far north as Helsinki, Finland. Upper Cook Inlet has the second greatest tide range in North America.

Although Alaska is vast, about half of the state's people live in or near Anchorage. Alaska, incidentally, has about 1 square mile for every resident.

Alaska contains more than half of the nation's parklands. These vast spans of land are home to unspoiled wilderness and countless wildlife. Many of the photographs and sketches of "Wild Alaska" are from these areas.

Alaska is one-fifth the size of the United States and also boasts more coastline than all the other states combined.

A band of Dall sheep graze on summer grasses in the mountains of the Alaska Range. During this time of year the ewes and lambs remain separated from the rams.

The northern lights (aurora borealis) are caused when the earth's upper atmosphere is bombarded by charged particles, resulting in a shimmering variety of colors and patterns. In Alaska, September to April are the prime viewing months.

Alaska's vast spans of marshes and wetlands are favorite nesting grounds for various migrating waterfowl.

Fire is a necessary requisite for a healthy landscape and for regenerating new vegetation growth. Although we now often fight forest fires vigorously when they threaten private property, we have also learned that allowing controlled burns on public land will greatly enhance wildlife habitat. Wildlife will gradually return to burned over areas to graze and browse on the new, nutritious growth.

The grizzly is a true indicator of wilderness. When the grizzly is gone, so, too, is the wilderness. Also, once removed, it is unlikely that people will allow it to be reintroduced back into the area due to its feared reputation.

There are over 10,000 glaciers in Alaska. Portage Glacier is one of the state's most visited attractions even though the glacier has greatly "retreated" during the past decade. Glaciers are ever moving; either retreating or advancing. The above photograph shows an iceberg floating in Portage Lake and the glacier in the background. Ice fields cover 28,000 square miles of Alaska.

Author's Journal *(August 22, '01)*

   Exit glacier. Near Seward. Colors are beginning to turn in the trees and on the hillsides. Splashes of reds and yellows mingle with the summer greens.

   The reason that glacier ice is so blue is because densely compacted ice absorbs the light spectrum's long wavelengths. Only shorter bluish wavelengths are reflected back for us to see.

Winter landscape

Author's Journal *(Jan. 4, '80)*
Of all the words one can conjure up about Alaska, there is none so apt or fitting as the word "awesome". It is powerful, gigantic, overwhelming, beautiful, inspiring and spectacular. But most of all it is downright awesome!

Colorful fireweed lines many of Alaska's highways during summer months. As summer progresses, the blooms climb higher and higher up the stem, until they finally reach the top. Many Alaskans say that winter is only six weeks away when fireweed tops out.

Left: Cotton grass, or "Alaska cotton", grows in bogs, wet meadows and along roadsides.
Right: A carpet of lilly pads blanket a small roadside pond near Moose Pass, Alaska, in late August.

The Totem poles of southeastern Alaska often tell stories or legends.

Fishing is an important industry in coastal Alaska. From this Kodiak harbor, fishermen pursue fish and crabs in unpredictably dangerous waters.

Old abandoned cabins are found scattered throughout the northcountry. Some were mining cabins, trapping cabins, or homesteads. Their small size, sturdy log walls and sod roofs made them easy to heat during the long, frigid winters. Nowadays, hikers often use them as shelter during inclement weather and share overnight quarters with the resident shrews, mice and even bats.

Alaska

is a paradise for outdoor sports and activities.

Busloads of tourists view Mount McKinley on a rare cloudless day. The winding road on the right leads to the scenic Wonder Lake area of Denali National Park.

Denali National Park is a place where tourists and residents are likely to see a wide variety of wildlife while riding the park's "shuttle buses". These buses were initiated some years ago in order to cut down on the private vehicles that were beginning to crowd the road and hence diminishing wildlife sightings. Bears (such as this sow and her cubs), wolves, fox and caribou are commonly seen walking the gravel road.

Bird Creek, south of Anchorage, is an example of where "combat fishing" (over-crowding, uncontrolled tempers and flying fishhooks are the ingredients) can occur. During the peak salmon runs of July and August, people fish shoulder-to-shoulder at the most popular spots.

My father, August, helps hold up a stringer of Russian River "reds" with the Brandvolds (Bruce, Sue, Joyce (my sister), and Lisa) in the 1980's.

King salmon are indeed the "king of salmon". The record fish weighs over 97 pounds.

A Dall ewe and lamb graze and browse along the hillsides overlooking the Seward highway and Alaska railroad. During the summer tourist-season, "sheep-jams" often occur along the narrow highway.

During late May, the "hooligan" runs begin and dipnetters head to the ocean's edge to scoop them up. Hooligan are small smelt-like fish that, besides being good eating, were also utilized as candles by Native Alaskans due to their oily nature.

Cameras are standard gear for most people who venture into Alaska's outdoors. Photographing wildlife helps to illustrate the "stories and adventures" that most of us tell one another.

Gold is one of the fabled words of Alaska's rich history. Recreational gold panners are often seen near roadside creeks trying to strike it rich or merely enjoying the experience. "Citico Charley" (shown here and one of the author's favorite "sourdough models") tries his luck on the Kenai Peninsula. Some years ago, prior to his death, he asked his family to scatter his ashes on Mount McKinley; saying "the view from there will be just fine".

Author's Journal *(Feb. 1, '82, Susitna Valley)*

Running into heavy snow on some of my trails and have to walk ahead of the dogs to break trail. Spooky is a good leader and will usually keep the team a few steps back from me and so isn't constantly stepping on the backs of my snowshoes the way Maruska does. She's one of those dogs that just can't seem to get "close enough", you know? I swear she should've been a cat instead of a dog! She's one of those dogs that seems to purr instead of bark.

Camping overnight in a stand of Spruce near the Little Susitna. Got the team chained and fed, set up the tent, rolled out two sleeping bags, and put the tea water on. Cold but not miserable if you're dressed for winter camping.

Ate stew, drank a pot of tea, and watched the stars overhead. An occasional flash of northern lights shimmered in the sky and an occasional owl hoot echoed through the stands of Spruce.

Fox and rabbit tracks are fairly scarce hereabouts, but moose tracks AND moose are everywhere it seems. I've had a couple of exciting rides through the woods when we ran up on a moose on our trail.

Left: A young Jenny Liska enjoys a dogsled ride with the author's 5-dog team in the 1970's.

Right: Dog mushing is Alaska's "state sport", and almost every type of dog conceivable has pulled sleds. Most sleddogs, however, usually have some mixture of husky or malamute mixed in.

A lone skier travels across the winter landscape. Hoarfrost covers the oceanside trees and brush.

Lowbush cranberries
(The red berries on the bushes are not cranberries)

After harvesting wild berries, many Alaskans add them to muffins and pancakes as well as cooking up various syrups, jellies and sauces.

Winter ice-climbing has become a very popular sport in Alaska during the past few years. Although ropes are often used, many daring people choose to free-climb these towering walls of ice.

Alaska
is a land of distinct seasons.

Spring is a season of birth and renewal. It is a time when the land and animals awake and bloom; a time when birds migrate North to their Alaska nesting grounds.

Dall ewe and week-old lamb / late May.

Winters in Alaska are long and food often becomes scarce. By early spring, moose have banded together on wind-swept flats where the hard packed snow makes for easier travel.

Author's Journal *(Apr. 25, '83, Kenai Peninsula)*
Snow geese everywhere lately. Huge flocks. Also, swans on the Moose river which I floated through and photographed without spooking. A lot of ducks and terns and one Snowy owl hunting the salt flats outside Kenai. It probably is on the prowl for sick and injured Snow or Canada geese.
Great to see the land once again awaken from the long sleep of winter.

Summer is a time when the land and animals of Alaska flourish under the warm temperatures and "endless" daylight hours. It is a season when the salmon runs peak; the berries and flowers grow and ripen; a time when the year's young grows and the adults regain their vigor.

Sockeye salmon turn a bright red color when they enter fresh water during spawning. The young fry migrate from their birth streams to the ocean, and in two or three years return to this same stream to "spawn" before then dying.

Author's Journal *(Aug. 7, '01, Seward)*

Spent the day near Seward photographing spawning salmon, Hiked a trail to Bear creek headwaters where a weir has been put up which enables the spawning salmon to be caught and their eggs retrieved and thereafter artificially raised at Trail lake hatchery. This greatly increases "survival" and the small fry are later reintroduced back into the wild.

I would <u>never</u> do that hike again without being "armed" with pepper spray. There was bear scat, tracks and partly-eaten salmon all over the area. After passing a few fresh piles of scat, I began to sing, clap and watch over my shoulder. There are a few large Brown bears that are hanging-out in the area as well as many less-threatening Black bears.

There were hundreds of Sockeyes trying to get through the weir and migrate upstream to spawn.

A half-year old grizzly cub peers down from the safety of his high perch. Although Black bears can climb trees throughout their lives, the Grizzly/Brown bear can only do it as a youth, as their relatively straight, long claws and heavy weight will restrict it from climbing as it gets older. However, large bears can still climb trees that have limbs which allow it to ascend and descend ladder-like.

Author's Journal (*Feb. 12, '79*)

State game biologists are planning to move about 40 upper Nelchina Basin Brown bears this coming spring.

The idea is to have them removed during the two or three weeks of moose calving in the area.

The belief is that bears are causing the 70% death rate of newborn moose. This experiment of moving the bears should either confirm or disprove this belief. An earlier project of thinning out the wolves in the area didn't seem to help prevent the high death rate amongst the area's moose calves. Therefore the Brown bear became the prime suspect.

During the two-year study, biologists attached radios to 122 newborn moose. Sixty-five of those calves died. Of these at least 52 were killed by bears. The rest died by either bears, wolves or various accidents.

Although the bears have a strong "homing" instinct and most will eventually return to their former range, they are being moved far enough that when they do return it will be after the "critical" period for moose calves.

Autumn is a time when the land begins to wind down and prepare for the upcoming winter. It is a time of vivid colors, of ripened berries, of "fattening up". The wild creatures that plan to winter in Alaska must utilize this season prudently. Those that don't will surely suffer or perish. It is also the season of migration south for the majority of bird species, as well as the season when many large mammals mate.

Author's Journal (*Sept. 12, '80, Fairbanks area*)
  Autumn comes to us with a sort of subtlety and yet with a sense of shock.
It is upon our first notice of a golden aspen leaf in the sea of green forest that
we realize summer has bid us adieu.

Left: A large rutting bull moose roams the colorful autumn hills of interior Alaska in pursuit of receptive mates. The area's strongest bull will often establish and breed a harem of cows. The task of keeping the cows "rounded up" and of fighting off challenging bulls, gives him little time to rest and feed. These bulls often enter the unforgiving winters in a state of weakness and malnutrition.

  Right: Wild blueberries ripen during the cooler days of autumn. Berry pickers must be ever alert for bears who are also scouring the hills in search of the berries.

Author's Journal (*Sept. 25, '83, Beaver Lake*)
  Days are getting shorter. Air is crisp. Termination dust (snow) is falling in
the high mountains and beginning its march downward. Overhead, waterfowl
passes, honking and squawking good-bye.

A pair of Dall rams in the Wrangell mountains. The larger ram is testing the air to determine the breeding receptivity of the band of ewes they are following. This "lip curl" is common in males of many species during the annual "rut".

Winters are a time of survival in Alaska's harsh climate. Only the hardiest and most adaptable birds and mammals can survive. Creatures such as the ptarmigan and Snowshoe hare change their coats to white to match the snowy terrain. Other creatures, such as the Arctic ground squirrel and Hoary marmot, must hibernate through the winter months. Still others, like the Collared pika, pile "haystacks" of plant cuttings throughout the summer months to sustain them through the winter.

The large browsing and grazing mammals must not only find adequate food under the deep snow, but must also evade the predators that constantly pursue them. Animals, such as Sitka blacktails, will now herd together to share the task of breaking trails and watching out for danger.

Author's Journal *(Jan. '75, Fish Creek)*

Was an even -50° F. early this morning. Records for cold weather are being set everyday all around Alaska. Many cities are reporting their lowest temperatures ever recorded for these dates. The cold snap may well last another 5 days according to the forecasters.

THIS is the time to live out in the "bush". Just throw an extra log in the fire and settle back. Plenty of hot tea, work, or books, until the "snap" passes. No electricity outages (as you have none), no having to get cars started, no having to plow through traffic in ice fog and carbon monoxide. Just settle back and wait while the rest of the world must keep things on schedule and the world turning.

Willow ptarmigan in winter plumage. Their white feathers also help in insulation, because white feathers have empty cells that are filled with air.

This Snowshoe hare relies on its camouflage as protection. However, when pursued by predators such as lynx and fox, its large hind paws often help propel it across the snowy terrain and to safety.

*B*ut above all,

Alaska is a land filled with magnificent and unique wildlife.

A Red fox patrols the woods of Elmendorf Air Force Base. Although the city of Anchorage has set aside numerous tracts for parks and refuges, it is the large tracts of undeveloped acreage of the two military bases outside the city that are home to much of the area's wildlife. Bears, moose, and fox are commonly seen in or near the city.

Although once abundant in Alaska, the muskoxen was killed off by hunters and explorers by the mid-1800's. A transplant from Canada reestablished small herds, and today, due to protection, they are expanding their range.

A bull caribou feeds on the tundra north of Cantwell, Alaska. The region's caribou have just recently shed their antler's "velvet" and the bulls are beginning to test one another with sparring matches.

Wildlife is often found near roads and care must therefore be taken so as not to run into them. Hundreds of moose, for instance, are killed each year from collisions with automobiles. Despite their often "tame" appearance, wildlife can prove dangerous if harassed or carelessly approached.

Canada geese are becoming too numerous in and near cities. Efforts are now being made to seek out nests and reducing the clutch of eggs to a single egg. By leaving the one egg will prevent the adult geese from laying another clutch. Also, pigs are sometimes used to reduce an area's eggs before their hatching.

A group of tourists enjoy watching a pair of young moose calves cross the road in Denali National Park to join their mother. An hour earlier the protective cow had aggressively chased away a young grizzly that had picked up their scent and was "testing" their vulnerability.

Brown/Grizzly bears roam throughout most of Alaska. The term "brown" commonly refers to coastal bears whereas the term "grizzly" commonly refers to members of this specie found in Alaska's interior. The coastal Brown bears have access to a rich diet of salmon and hence can often exceed 1400 pounds.

WILDLIFE OF ALASKA

This book is not intended to show "all" of Alaska's wildlife, but rather those that are most familiar and those that the Alaska resident or visitor is most likely to see.

Few places on earth house such a varied array of creatures as does Alaska, America's "Last Frontier". Unique and colorful birds and mammals roam the forests, seasides, mountains and meadows, and it has been my pleasure to follow, photograph and draw them for over thirty years.

Although I now live in Anchorage, I have lived for many years in Alaska's "bush". Out there, away from towns and roads, I was able to work on my art and also to observe wildlife and nature. It was a period of solitude and reflection, and the serenity of these various wilderness settings are memories that will live with me forever.

Hopefully the following pages may be educational and enjoyable. I have added a few random journal entries to let the reader partially share these wildlife encounters and wilderness experiences with me.

Author's Journal *(March 8, '73, Mankomen Lake)*

"Windows of Wildlife" are these. From these cabin windows I have watched grizzlies, moose, caribou, wolves, fox, mink, wolverine, and all other odds n' ends of wildlife parading about their domain. I have watched cock ptarmigan fighting their aerial spring-time battles across the lake; I have watched Peregrine falcons and Bald eagles baited down to an old moose bone tossed out on the frozen lake. I have laid in bed and watched the northern lights dance across the sky or watch a fox nibble on Chinook's bowl of Friskies. I have seen ravens dive at moose and bears; have watched caribou swimming the lake, their hollow hairs making them amongst the best of swimmers. Whistling swans and hoards of Sandhill cranes have passed over every autumn, as I sat inside painting or perhaps sipping on a hot cup of tea.

All this has happened and all this I have watched through these cabin windows; these "windows of wildlife." No Hollywood movie could even remotely compare with this "show of shows."

Northern lights

BIRDS
OF
ALASKA

Alaska is home to a varied array of birds, from the majestic white-headed Bald eagle to the small, colorful warblers and hummingbirds. It is a land where "resident" birds like the ptarmigan change their feather colors to match the seasons, and where "tourist" birds like the Arctic tern travel thousands of miles to, in order to nest and raise families before again migrating "outside" to enjoy a more temperate winter climate. It is a land of diverse terrain, long summer days and abundant prey. It is, in essence, a land that will appeal to many species for a few months of every year. However, only the hardiest of birds are able to survive the frigid, long winters of Alaska.

The following section is of the "Birds of Alaska". It is a portfolio of many of Alaska's favorite and/or familiar birds.

Author's Journal *(April 27, '74, Beaver Lakes country)*
There were a couple of new "bird songs" in the woods today. Didn't see any of the traveling minstrels but their shrill notes floated through the snow-covered woods and seemed to bring with them a note of urging demands. They, too, seem to be disgusted with this lingering winter scene. The Northland is restless, anxious to get on with its job of bearing and raising a family.

Alaska is estimated to have over 20,000 nesting pairs of Bald eagles.

Bald eagle

Bald eagle

Chick

**Immature
Bald eagle**

Author's Journal *(Aug. 23, '74, Mt. Marathon, near Seward, Alaska)*

Clouds moved in across Resurrection Bay this morning. Still hot. Went back up to a Bald eagle's nest and shared an eaglet's first flight.

I was laying in a little clearing across from the nest when the eaglet began to test his wings and his courage by jumping up to a dead limb 5 feet above the nest. This jump was made with the assistance of a bit of clumsy wing flapping. And then, with seemingly only a momentary pause for a quick glance over his domain, he leaned forward, lifted his wings, and then with a downward thrust of his wings he left the dead limb. With wings stretched and flapping, he glided down the slope and into a new world.

I did search for him later but was unable to locate him due to the thick foliage. I'm sure his parents will locate and continue to feed him until he can return to the nest or fend for himself. (It is often said that eagle parents will starve the young eagles out of the nest and into taking their first flight. After a few days with no food, the eaglets instincts drive them from the nest in search of it.)

This afternoon, as I lay on the hillside, I watched the birds glide effortlessly through the sky; the majestic adult Bald eagles with their snowy heads and tails; the chattering Black-billed magpies; the sea gulls drifting in the drafts above Resurrection Bay. What a wondrous thing–flight! I thought of that eaglet with his first flight. What had pushed him off that dead limb? Instinct? The thrill of the unknown? I well remember my first Army paratrooper jump. Can I identify with that daring young eaglet? Perhaps not, but it suits me to think I can.

Salmon and other fish are a Bald eagle's main diet.

A late salmon run in the Chilkat river (near Haines, Alaska) will often attract a few thousand Bald eagles.

Author's Journal *(Nov. 22, '78, enroute to Haines)*

Left home heading north. Weather turned absolutely lousy towards Willow and Talkeetna and I fought a blizzard and icy roads for the next 300 miles. Roads up Fairbanks way were nasty too, having snowed there the past few days.

Heading to Tok, then down to Haines to photograph the "gathering of Bald eagles" that normally occurs thereabouts about this time.

Author's Journal *(Nov. 24, '78, Haines area)*

Lotsa "Baldies" around. Must have seen some 500 to 1,000 Bald eagles today. Went walking along the rivers hereabouts most of the day. A slight drizzle fell on and off.

A lot of buffleheads and goldeneyes in the bays here; all swimming around in huge "rafts."

Peaceful night. Sitting here across the bay from Haines watching the little town's lights sparkle and dance on the rippling ocean. Nice town, nice people.

Adult

Spawned-out Sockeye salmon (male)

"Where Eagles Soar"

"Proud Alaskan"

The Bald eagle is so named for its conspicuous white head. An adult Bald eagle doesn't sport its white head (and tail) until about 5 years of age. Until then it is often mistaken for a Golden eagle (see the immature eagle on page 39). Adults have wing spans of about 7 feet and normally weigh about 10 to 14 pounds. Females are larger than males. Nesting begins in April and normally two chicks are born.

Alaska used to have a bounty on Bald eagles and many thousands were killed before the bounty was removed in 1953. Since then, the Bald eagle has recovered in Alaska, but is still considered threatened in the "lower 48".

Author's Journal *(Aug. 4, '79, Beaver Lakes)*
There is, I believe, no more fierce independent look than that held in the eye of an eagle.

President Kennedy once said of the Bald eagle. "The fierce beauty and proud independence of this great bird aptly symbolized the strength and freedom of America."

Golden eagles are so named because of the "golden" feathers that adults have on their necks (see photograph below for illustration). Adult eagles have wing spans of over 6 feet and average 8 to 12 pounds. They are superb hunters. Prey includes hares, ground squirrels, marmots and other small mammals and birds. They, like Bald eagles, will also feed on carrion. Nesting usually occurs on rocky cliffsides.

Over the years they have suffered the same fate as other large birds of prey; that is, they have been poisoned, shot, and misunderstood. Often persecuted as "lamb killers", the majestic Golden eagle is a rare sight in areas where it once flourished. Hopefully, education and strict laws will help protect these needed predators.

Golden eagle (adult).

Author's Journal *(June 1, '71, Mt. McKinley Nat'l Park)*

Early this afternoon I sat on a hillside and watched as a Golden eagle swept down out of the mountain sky and killed a marmot that was sunning himself on a rocky ridge, not knowing it was under attack until the moment before the eagle hit it. The marmot had been careless, and here in this savage land of predators, it has cost him his life. Perhaps it is the species way of removing its unwary and hence unsuitable from their genetic line.

It was the way of predator and prey. And today, up here in the highcountry, it was all explained seemingly just for me.

✷✷Note: In my journal entries I sometimes refer to Denali National Park as Mt. McKinley National Park, because that was its former name during those entry dates.

The majestic Golden eagle breeds from Alaska east across northern Canada and south to Mexico. In parts of their range where prey is plentiful, the eagles will not migrate but remain year 'round. Alaska's Golden eagles normally leave for more temperate climates in late autumn because mainstay prey such as marmots and ground squirrels have hibernated for the winter.

Hoary marmots are a frequent prey animal of the Golden eagle.

Golden eagles

Birds of prey are not social animals and so are very territorial, in that they will aggressively defend a particular area. These birds hold territories for a variety of reasons. It helps to guarantee a food supply of prey and it also ensures fidelity between mating pairs as all intruding rivals are driven off.

Left: the Swainson's hawk has larger, more pointed wings than other "buteos" (broad-winged hawks) such as the more common Red-tailed hawk. Its plumage varies greatly, making it a difficult bird to identify. Its hunting technique is to soar above open areas before descending upon its spotted prey.

Right: The Northern goshawk is our largest accipiter (short-winged, long-tailed hawks), and can easily weave its way through dense woodlands to pursue its prey. The larger female is similar in coloring to the male. Mature birds have red eyes.

Opposite: Raptors are predators that must hunt and kill other animals in order to live. Alaska raptors include eagles, falcons, hawks, owls and osprey. All are equipped with magnificent eyesight, superb flying abilities, sharp talons and beaks.

The Red-tailed hawk shown here illustrates its large eyes, powerful talons and sharp beak. When a raptor's legs are extended, its clawed toes are spread wide. Upon impact, the legs buckle and the talons close, impaling the prey.

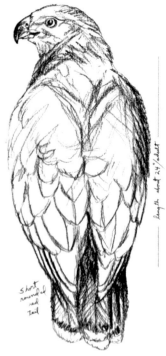

Red-tailed hawk

**Red-tailed hawk
(Buteo jamaicensis)
Length: 20-25"**

The Red-tailed hawk is a large hawk with a 4 foot wingspan. Their coloration varies, and the breasts of adult birds may be white, reddish, or brown. They often soar in wide circles while searching for prey such as hares, squirrels and ground-feeding birds such as ptarmigan and grouse. They normally nest in trees, but cliffs are also used. The most widespread member of the genus Buteo, their "keeeer" scream is heard throughout most of North America.

The Gyrfalcon is the largest of the true falcons and may measure 4 feet from wingtip to wingtip. It breeds on the tundra of northern Alaska and Canada and may live year 'round in the same area, hunting wary ptarmigan and assorted migratory birds that have ventured north to nest. Its voice is a screaming "kaak-kaak-kaak".

Peregrine falcon
(Falco peregrinus)
Length: 15-20"

Wingspan 3-3½ feet

Wings, tail & body are heavily barred

Peregrine falcon

Peregrine falcons

Gyrfalcon

Often called the "duck hawk", the Peregrine falcon is perhaps the world's speediest hunter, often diving at speeds of 180 mph. Although still rare outside Alaska, this magnificent bird is slowing reestablishing itself across North America. It nests on cliff ledges and hunts mostly birds such as ducks, gamebirds, and shorebirds.

A mallard drake flushes after sighting a circling falcon, therby giving the hunter a chance to knock it out of the sky.

Peregrine falcons

The Merlin ("Pigeon hawk") is a small jay-sized falcon. The backs of males are slate colored and the females are brown. Their long tail is boldly banded. Nests in tree cavities and on rocky ledges. Its prey is insects and small birds.

American kestrel

"Sparrow hawks" share the task of building the nest, but the female alone incubates the eggs and cares for the chicks. The male is the primary hunter for the family. Nests in tree cavities and has a shrill "killie-killie" cry.

**American kestrel
(Falco sparverius)
Length: 10-12"
Wingspan: 20-22"**

Author's Journal *(April 27, '78, Goose Bay)*

I'm impressed! Saw 100's of swans bunched up throughout Goose Bay (near Knik, Alaska). Also lots of ducks and geese.

Would imagine this area to be a resting and gathering spot for the waterfowl before they head north to their own particular nesting sites. Hope to spend the next few days crawling around out here with my camera.

Saw a Sparrow hawk out south of Palmer with a small bird in its talons. Also, at Goose Bay, as I was perched up on a ridge watching the waterfowl, a Bald eagle flew over the Bay and every (seemingly) duck and goose in the area seemed to rise and take wing. Boy, what terror those birds of prey must bring!

The American kestrel (or Sparrow hawk), is identifiable by its small size and reddish tail and back. It is able to hover above its prey before striking. Insects and small rodents and birds are its primary diet.

Barred tail

Although it is illegal to kill any bird of prey in Alaska, it is still estimated that a significant number are shot. Of course, as with other wildlife, a certain number also die needlessly and often painfully by getting tangled up in carelessly discarded monofilament fishing line and hooks.

**Osprey
(Pandion haliaetus)
Length: 19-24"
Wingspan 5-6'**

Salmon

The Osprey is a brown and white, long-winged "fish hawk". It lives and nests near water where its prey dwells. When fishing, the Osprey dives with its talons bared, striking the water with great force and impaling its quarry. Its white head with dark eye stripe helps identify it.

The Osprey is unique and the sole member of the family Pandionidae. Their nests are usually a bulky structure of sticks which it adds to yearly.

Great Horned Owl

Although considered strictly nocturnal creatures, here in the far North the owls have been known to "operate" almost around the clock during the nesting season. They nest earlier than most birds, (January-February) and their young are often hunting by the time their prey's young is born and thus vulnerable.

Great Horned owls: Length 18-26 inches; wingspan 46-60 inches. Their call is a distinctive "hooo" sound. Nests in deserted hawk or raven nests, tree cavities, as well as other varied places. Hares, birds, and small mammals are usual fare. Two to four chicks is a common clutch.

Chick

Author's Journal *(May 9, '81, Big Lake area)*

Just found a Great Horned owl's nest. I was out looking for Spruce grouse (their mating season) and Sandhill cranes (they have really been squawking up a ruckus hereabouts these past few days) and just chanced upon seeing an owl while glassing a single Sandhill crane feeding in a marsh (there had been 3 earlier, but two must've paired off leaving this third one alone for the present). There are 3 little "snowballs" (chicks) huddled together in a former raven's nest (raven's nested there last year).

Adult

GREAT HORNED OWL
CHICKS
6-8 WEEKS

Showshoe hare (winter coat)

The Great Horned owl is the most common owl in Alaska. This efficient predator is very protective of its nesting area and will often swoop down and attack humans that venture too near its nest or young. In Alaska's arctic, it is almost white in color to match its environment. Its large size, prominent ear tufts and bright yellow eyes are distinguishing features.

Snowshoe hares are a primary prey animal. Also, when their population soars, so do the number of owl chicks raised.

Defense pose

Showshoe hare (spring coat)

A young Great Horned owl chick has recently left its nest and has spent the past day clumsily testing its wings. If threatened, it will fluff up its feathers and click its beak (see opposite page) in an attempt to scare off the intruder.

Snowy Owl

Female

The Snowy owl is one of Alaska's most beautiful owls. The male is almost pure white, while the female Snowy owl has dark colored bars scattered over its body. This round-headed, 2-foot-tall owl has a wing spread of 4 to 5 feet.

The Snowy owl nests in northern Alaska and depends primarily on lemmings for its diet, although larger mammals and birds are sometimes acquired. A ground-nester, the number of eggs hatched is also influenced by its food supply. When prey is scarce, the "ghost owl" migrates south to areas where prey is adequate.

Lemming

True lemmings are restricted to tundra habitats in Alaska. They undergo cyclical populations depending upon the available food supplies.

Male

Author's Journal *(Oct. 28, '79, Beaver Lakes)*

6" of snow fell last night. Winter Wonderland. Trees are drooping with thick white blankets. Lake has a slushy ice covering about half-way out.

A huge flock of about 200 goldeneyes on the lake today.

A great day here in the north country. Went walking.

Someone once said that there are some who can live without wild things and some who cannot. I certainly cannot.

To be the sole owner of all that passes beneath one's feet, unbounded and unshackled in spirit, that is the beauty of walking Alaska's wilds.

Male

Snowy owls

Female

Great Gray owl

**Young
Hawk owl**

**Great Gray owl
(Strix nebulosa)
Length: 2 to 3 feet
Wingspan: 5 feet**

**Hawk owl
(Surnia ulula)
Length: 14-17"
Wingspan: 2 1/2- 3 feet**

Great Gray owl (adult)

Red squirrel

Hawk owl

The Short-eared owl is a ground nester, while the Hawk owl and Screech owl usually nest in tree cavities. The larger Great Gray owl nests high in trees.

In Alaska, small mammals make up a large part of small owl's diet. Red squirrels, ground squirrels, lemmings and mice are "favorites".

Short-eared owl

Screech owl

Arctic ground squirrel

The small Boreal owl hunts mostly during the night. During the daylight hours, this 10 to 12" owl conceals itself in dense foliage or tree holes. Because it, like other owls, has downy edged primary wing feathers, it can swoop down on its prey silently. It and the smaller Saw-Whet owl are often mistaken for one another.

The Screech owl is another small Alaska owl. It, and the Northern Pygmy owl, seldom ventures north of southeastern Alaska; whereas the Boreal and Saw-Whet owls are commonly found in central Alaska.

Pygmy owl

Boreal owl

Saw-Whet owls

Author's Journal *(Feb. 6, '79, Beaver Lakes country)*
    Spent the better part of the morning following a Boreal owl around the woods. Firstly spotted him as I walked out on the lake ice for my morning look up and down the lake. He was so intent on hunting shrews at my woodpile that I walked within an arm's length of him. Only when I said "Good Morning Big Eyes" did he pivot his head and give me a few seconds of attention.
    Hope he got his morning's "ham and eggs" (shrews).
    A thought. Wilderness air: so fresh and clean, as though nobody's ever used it before.

The Western screech-owl is a small, mottled owl that has ear "tufts" (laid flat on this photo). It lives and hunts the woodlands and meadows for mice and voles. Because it hunts prey whose populations may fluctuate greatly, it incubates each egg as it is laid. Therefore the eggs hatch in sequence and the brood varies widely in size and age. If prey is scarce, then only the older chicks will survive.

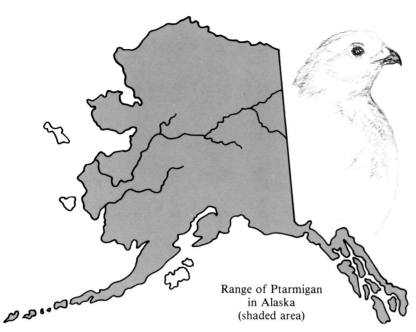

Range of Ptarmigan
in Alaska
(shaded area)

Willow ptarmigan

The
PTARMIGAN
in Alaska

The Willow ptarmigan above, begins to turn his brown summer feathers into its white winter coat. The Rock ptarmigan below, is turning his white winter feathers into its summer camouflaging attire.

Rock ptarmigan

bright red eyebrow

swollen neck while proclaiming his territory with a series of gargling and croaking noises. Mid-May plummage.

Ptarmigan: The ptarmigan are close relatives of the grouse. Alaska has three kinds of ptarmigan: Willow, Rock, and White-tailed. They weigh about 1 pound, their toes and legs are feathered, and they turn white to match the winter's snow. Ground nesters: 6 to 10 eggs usually hatch in June. Their population seems to run in cycles and is influenced by weather conditions also.

Willow ptarmigan

Male / spring

The Willow ptarmigan is Alaska's state bird.

Author's Journal *(Sept. 1, '77, Moose Pass area)*

Went roaming today. Flushed a few covies of ptarmigan, usually sending the mother bird into her broken-wing act. Feigning a broken wing, the mother is usually able to lure most predators away from her hidden chicks, by seemingly offering herself as an "easy catch". Just about the time the predator thinks he has her, she just ups and flies away, leaving the bewildered fox (or whatever) standing there with his mouth agape, wondering just what in the dickens happened to his sure meal. Meanwhile, the hen and her clutch of chicks are now far away and safe.

Since the chicks can surely fly by now, I wonder why this charade continues? Perhaps it's hard for a mother to finally admit that her children have indeed grown up and no longer need her to fight their every battle. Few mothers have the heart to pull in their "apron strings" before they absolutely have to.

Winter coat

Author's Journal *(May 13-16, '82, Denali Nat'l Park)*

First 1982 trip to my favorite country of Denali. Still a lot of snow in the area but it should melt fast.

The ptarmigan are setting up their territories again. The cocks seem to all be strategically located in the best spots so as to keep an eye on their little kingdom and to keep all intruders out.

There is a lot of cackling and dog-fighting going on in the area; different species of birds protecting their nesting grounds.

Author's Journal *(Jan. 26, '71, Nenana area)*
We have been having a barrage of Northern Lights filled nights lately. Usually between 10 P.M. and 3 A.M. is the best time to watch their dancing, dazzling display. In the early 1900's polar explorer Frederick Cook wrote that the aurora made him "spiritually intoxicated". Photographing ptarmigan.

Willow ptarmigan

As the snows of early autumn descend upon interior Alaska, the foliage begins to change colors before dying and falling to the ground. The Willow ptarmigan also begins to change its colors to match the white of the approaching winter landscape.

The GROUSE in Alaska

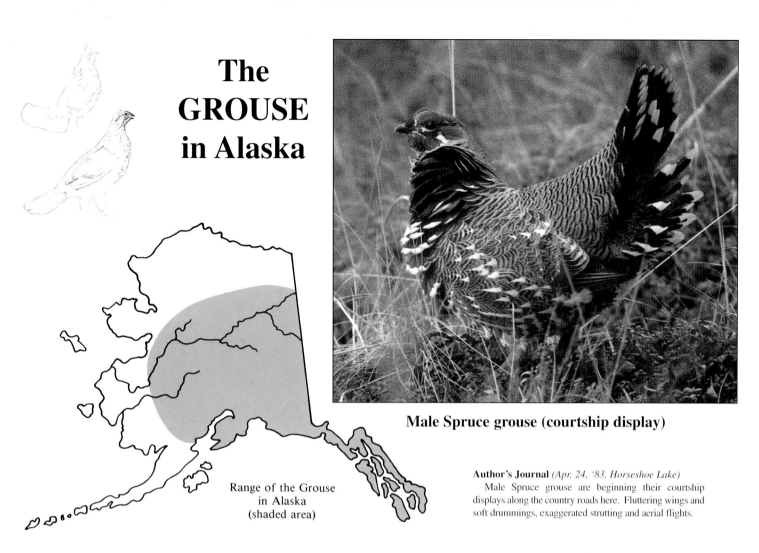

Male Spruce grouse (courtship display)

Range of the Grouse
in Alaska
(shaded area)

Author's Journal *(Apr. 24, '83, Horseshoe Lake)*
Male Spruce grouse are beginning their courtship displays along the country roads here. Fluttering wings and soft drummings, exaggerated strutting and aerial flights.

Spruce grouse (autumn)

Ruffed grouse

Spruce

Blue

Spruce

Ruffed

The grouse is often referred to as the Alaskan "chicken". Feathers cover the nostrils and lower legs. The hens usually nest in May; a usual batch of 6 to 12 eggs is laid in a shallow ground nest.

The Alaskan grouse include the Blue grouse of Southeastern as well as the Spruce, Ruffed and Sharp-tailed grouse that are also found further north. The Blue grouse (or "hooter") is Alaska's largest upland game bird - with the males weighing 3 or 4 pounds.

The males of all the grouse species have flamboyant courtship displays; including "drumming", "booming", and all sorts of fancy dances. The males, also, do not incubate or help rear the young.

Great Gray Owl

Spruce grouse occur throughout Alaska. Their usual habitat is a treed land with an understory of berries and mosses. Insects, berries and vegetation make up their summer diet, but during the winter months they exist almost totally on spruce needles.

During the May mating period, the drumming of the males rapidly beating wings can often be heard. It is also a time when the males are more vulnerable to predators, such as owls.

The Ruffed grouse is a brownish-gray, chicken-like bird with a small crest, black-banded tail, and blackish "ruffs" on its neck. Often nests in a shallow depression lined with leaves and hidden under a bush or tree.

The male's spring mating ritual includes his finding a favorite log from which he beats the air with his wings, creating a drumming noise that rapidly increases in tempo.

The Blue grouse is Alaska's largest grouse with a length of up to 21 inches. It nests in coniferous forests, muskegs and alpine meadows.

During the spring mating season the male can "display" by bending its neck feathers to show their white bases while revealing the yellow-red skin beneath. Also, large combs over the eyes can be changed in color from yellow to brilliant red.

A Spruce grouse (from this year's hatch) pauses from its berry feeding to watch a Red squirrel feed on spruce cones nearby. Since they are not known as a very cautious bird, few young survive until the coming spring.

HORNED PUFFIN & TUFTED PUFFIN

Puffins are perhaps Alaska's "favorite" birds. These colorful seabirds spend most of their lives on the open sea and only come to land during the summer's breeding season. It is also during this period that their colors of oranges, reds, blacks and whites are the most striking.

Puffins normally nest underground. In May they arrive at their nesting sites and lay a single egg, an egg incubated by both parents for a period of 1-1/2 months until its hatching. Once hatched, the chick hides in the burrow until both parents return from their fishing trips. If it ventures out, it is susceptible to attacks by predators such as gulls and fox.

Two species of puffins occur in Alaska: the Horned puffin and the Tufted puffin. Both weigh over 1 pound and stand about 12-14" tall. The Horned puffin sports a white breast while the Tufted puffin sports tufts of feathers on both sides of its head and has a black body. Both have bills colored in reds and yellows.

Horned puffins

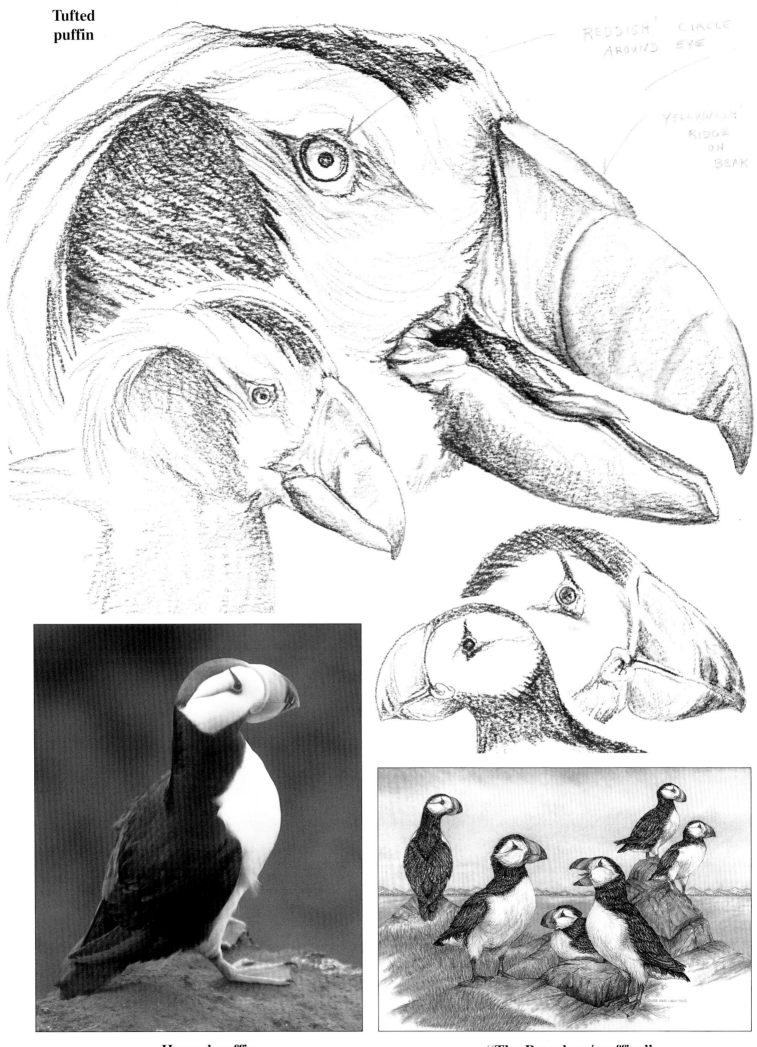

Tufted puffin

REDDISH CIRCLE AROUND EYE

YELLOWISH RIDGE ON BEAK

Horned puffin

"The Preacher / puffins"

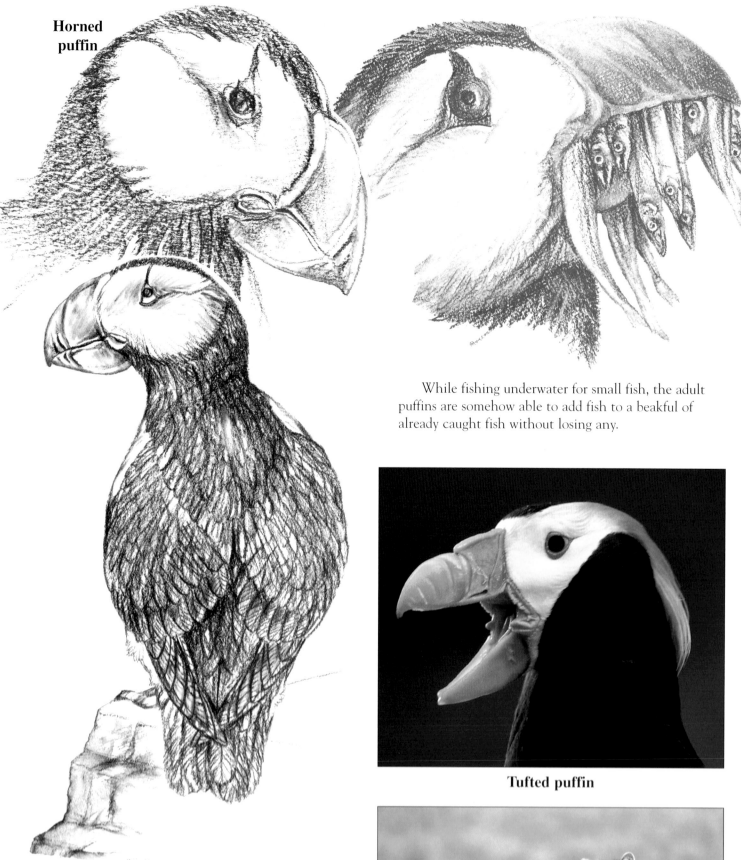

Horned puffin

While fishing underwater for small fish, the adult puffins are somehow able to add fish to a beakful of already caught fish without losing any.

Tufted puffin

Arctic fox

Author's Journal *(June 16, '74, Pribilof Islands, Bering Sea)*

Flew out to the Pribilof Islands yesterday. St. Paul Island (one of them) is only some 30 square miles in size, but is the breeding home to thousands of fur seals as well as nesting grounds for over 100 different species of birds. Unbelievable place!

Followed a fox on his round today. He was busily killing birds along the steep rookeries. I witnessed him kill one murre and three kittiwakes. The birds are "sitting ducks" for a fox. He simply makes a short charge into a batch of nesting birds and kills one, which he then "caches" for pickup later (or perhaps never) or takes home to his family.

One kittiwake kill was taken home for the young fox kits to play with, tear up and finally eat. They were certainly not famished as they seemed just as happy for a new plaything as they did for a tasty meal.

The bird rookeries, incidentally, are on sheer cliffs which sometimes rise 200 feet above the sea. A person walking the cliff edge must be ever on the alert for a "weak shoulder" on the ledge. One careless step could easily result in a sure death on the rocks far below.

Arctic loon

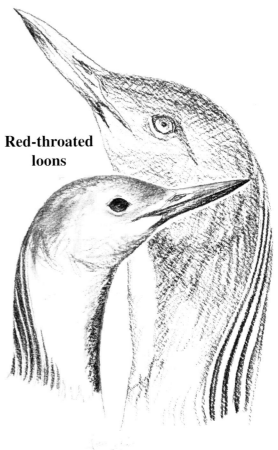

Red-throated loons

LOONS
in Alaska

All five species of the world's loons are found in Alaska. They are the Common, Red-throated, Yellow-billed, Pacific and Arctic.

Normally two eggs are laid in May or June on a lake's shoreline or island edge. Because of predation and nest disturbance, usually only half the chicks survive to migrate south.

The "cry" of the loon is a true wilderness sound, and the abundance of the birds around Alaska is proof of the pristine quality of its waters. The flight of loons can be identified by their low-slung head and neck.

Common loon

Common loon

Author's Journal *(May 2, '81, Beaver Lakes)*
    This morning, while munching grapefruit at my kitchen table overlooking
the lake, 6 Trumpeter swans glided by and put down at the north end of the lake.
    The first 2 loons of the year were yodeling throughout last night.

Common loons (Gavia immer) have dark blackish-green heads and necks, white chests, and a black back spotted with white. Both male and female loons are marked similarly. Loons mate for life and return every year to the same nesting area.

The dragonfly is Alaska's "state insect". It feeds mainly on mosquitoes, of which twenty-five species live in Alaska. The dragonfly often falls prey to gulls and various other birds.

The Mew gull is a small gull that nests along lakeshores and the seacoast from Alaska east into central Canada. An adult's coloring is white with a gray mantle, black wing tips, and greenish-yellow legs. Its voice is a high mewing "kee-yeer".

Mew gulls lay 2 or 3 olive-colored eggs in a grass nest near water. The spotted gray chicks are fed regurgitated fish, etc., until they can fend for themselves. The trio of chicks shown here show patience as they await a passing insect or small fish.

Golden plover

Long-tailed jaeger

Long-tailed jaegers nest on
tundra and rocky hillsides. Insects
and lemmings are common prey.

Killdeer
Its call is "kill-dee, kill-dee".

Left: Black-billed magpie. Nests in tall bushes.

Right: Common raven. Nests on cliffs or in trees. Magpies, ravens and crows are some of the bird kingdom's
smartest members and are common throughout much of Alaska.

Right: A Lesser yellowlegs stands about 7" tall and is similarly colored to the 10" tall Greater yellowlegs. Yellowlegs migrate south in September and winter from Washington to South America.

Their long legs allow it to feed in or at water's edge.

Curlew

Arctic tern chick

GREAT BLUE HERON

Arctic terns make a yearly 25,000 mile round-trip between their winter home in the Antarctic and their Alaskan nesting grounds. The graceful birds are expert fishermen, hovering over a spot until their aquatic prey is sighted and dove for.

The forked tail, red bill and black-capped head distinguishes the Arctic tern.

Common murres / Pribilof Islands

    Common murres are seabirds found along Alaska's coasts and islands. Their white and black coats make them look like "little penguins", a specie not found in Alaska.

    Murres nest on rocky cliffs and ledges and lay a single egg. In late summer the young chicks will plummet from their birth site to the sea far below. Seabirds such as puffins and murres are extremely vulnerable to oil spills and pollution, due to spending most of their lives in water.

Long-tailed jaegers will aggressively protect their nesting grounds from any intruder.

A Red-necked grebe readjusts its clutch of eggs. Nests are commonly built on the edges of shallow ponds and lakes and on vegetation that allows the nest to float. This book's author formerly lived on a small lake that usually housed 8 to 12 grebe families every summer.

Dancing Crane
Fairbanks, Alaska
2001

Sandhill cranes (Grus canadensis) are wading birds that have long necks, long black legs and stand about 3 feet tall. Adults are a grayish color and have a bright red forehead.

Except for the solitary nesting season, cranes are very social birds and often feed together as well as roost together. They are very wary and by grouping together are able to share watching for predators. Their diet consists of insects, seeds, frogs, rodents and sometimes grain. In Alaska's farming communities, large flocks of cranes often congregate to feed.

Those that enjoy watching birds are often fascinated by the seemingly joyous and carefree mating "dances" that the adults perform for one another. These exaggerated dances of bowing, hopping and flapping of wings can go on for long periods. Although this ritual is most often displayed during early spring, it occurs throughout the year when two or more cranes meet.

Sandhill crane

Unlike herons, cranes fly with their necks outstretched.

The Sandhill crane migrates to and from Alaska in flocks, but the individual pairs will scatter widely when choosing their nesting site. Nesting occurs in May and usually two spotted-brown eggs are laid. Both parents tend the nest until the chicks are born in about a month.

Sandhill crane chick / June

SWANS
in Alaska

Trumpeter swans

Two species of swans nest in Alaska: the Trumpeter and the Tundra ("whistling") swan. Adult birds are pure white and immature young are a gray color. Tundra swans are about 2/3's the size of the Trumpeter's 20-30 pound range, and usually can be distinguished by a yellow spot between their black bill and eye.
Note: the Whooper swan is a rare occurence in Alaska and may nest to a very limited extent here.

Trumpeter swans have a deep, horn-like call, while the call of the Tundra swan is a high "whoop".

Although the swans are no longer listed as "endangered", they are, nevertheless, rare in much of America. Alaska, it is estimated, houses most of the world's nesting pairs. Most Trumpeter swans winter from southeastern Alaska to Washington.

Swans normally mate for life and usually will nest by their fourth year. Huge nests are built at water's edge and three or four (average) eggs are incubated for about a month before the "cygnets" are hatched. The diet of swans includes seeds, tubers, pondweeds and grain.

A mating pair of Trumpeter swans begin nesting early in the spring, a time when there is still snow and ice.

Trumpeter swan

Whooper swan

Alaska's three species of swans are shown here (adults).

Tundra swan

Author's Journal *(April 19, '75, Kenai area)*

Counted 21 Trumpeters in a short stretch of the Moose river. They are America's largest waterfowl; really gigantic (especially if they're winging over you at about 12 feet or so).

Earlier, after seeing and hearing ravens on a bend of the Kenai river, I hiked down and found them feeding on a moose carcass. Two Bald eagles were perched in the trees above and a Red fox kept running at and scattering the ravens as he fed on a scrap nearby.

Trumpeter swan chick

In the mid-1930's there were less than 100 Trumpeter swans world-wide. Now, 70 years later, there are over 13,000 swans in Alaska alone.

A bird's feathers must be kept in a healthy and clean condition. Preening and washing are a crucial daily task.

The Tundra swan is smaller than the Trumpeter swan and its call is more of a "hoo-ha-hoo" than the bugling "ko-hah" of the Trumpeter. A small yellowish spot in front of its eye also helps distinguish it.

The CANADA GOOSE in Alaska

Range of Canada Geese
in Alaska
(shaded area)

Canada goose

Canada geese (Branta canadensis). There are 6 subspecies of Canada geese that occur in Alaska. They range in size from the duck-sized Cackling goose to the large (15#) Vancouver goose. They are readily identified by their white rumps and cheeks and by their long, black necks. Most also "honk". Canada geese mate for life and hatching often occurs in early June. The year's young join the parents for the autumn migration south and the plentiful "v's" of geese overhead in October is a sure sign that Alaska's winter is not far behind.

Normally 4 to 6 goslings are born per nest. Later, families often combine their young into large groups, which allow the adults more time to feed by sharing "babysitting duties" with other adults.

86

Canada geese

Author's Journal *(May 30, '81, Potter's flats)*

Baby goslings are born. Saw three sets of adults with chicks. A few pair were still seemingly without. Did see a Red fox on the east side of the marsh–could mean trouble for the geese–but then, so is the nature of nature's children. Some live and some die so others may live.

A pair of Marsh hawks patrolled the shoreline until being driven out by a few pair of nesting terns.

Common characteristics of Canada geese are: similar male and female coloration, and being very social birds (except during nesting). Vegetation and crops make up the bulk of their diet. Foxes, coyotes, gulls and ravens are major predators of eggs, goslings, and even adults.

Geese usually mate for life.

Canada goose

The GEESE in Alaska

Four other geese species, besides Canada geese, are found in Alaska. They are Emperor, Whitefront, lesser Snow, and Black brant. Although the Ross goose, Bean goose, Blue goose, and Atlantic brant are sighted occasionally, they are considered a rare resident.

White-Fronted goose

Author's Journal *(April 26, '80, Kenai Peninsula)*
Snow geese peaked around April 22 here on the Kenai. Most have already departed for Siberia.

Snow geese

Huge flocks of Snow geese often congregate to feed on the Kenai tide-flats before continuing their springtime migration to their northern nesting grounds.

Chick

The colorful Emperor goose commonly winters on Alaska's Aleutian Islands. It is a seldom seen specie as it spends most of its life in areas not frequented by humans. Females are already bred by the time they arrive at their nesting grounds in May. A ground nester, they must protect their eggs and young from the tundra's predators such as Arctic foxes, gulls and jaegers. Their diet consists of grasses, berries, shellfish and seaweed. Its body is silvery-gray and its head, hindneck, and tail are white. Their bill is pink and their feet are orange.

The King eider nests in remote regions of the Arctic. Males sport a very conspicuous yellow-orange bill while the females are a mottled brown. The eiders migrate to or from their nesting grounds in huge flocks; usually in separate flocks of either males or females.

The Common eider is our largest duck. The male is a combination of blacks and whites, whereas the female is the brownish coloration of many hens. Both have long, sloping bills. Nesting colonies are sometimes established in certain regions of the coast. Also, the "down" the hens use to line their nest is often harvested by Natives after the year's hatching, as it is used to insulate garments.

The colorful Green-winged teal (male) is commonly seen in marshes and ponds across much of Alaska. Males make a repeated whistle sound and the females quack.

Author's Journal (*May 15, '77*)

Set up a small blind at Potter's Flats (south of Anchorage) today. There are always a lot of ducks and geese swimming around out there and I thought a blind might help me sneak a few photos.

Spent about 2 hours building the blind, not caring that all the birds left during my building session. Once the blind was up and I was hidden inside, new flocks of passing ducks and geese would land and paddle by.

The Hooded merganser is a small duck with a slender pointed bill. The male (shown) has a white, black-bordered crest, a white breast (with two black stripes down side), and tannish-rust flanks. The female is a grayish-brown color. Their call is a series of chatters and grunts. Normally nest in a down-lined tree cavity or in a fallen hollow log. Their diet consists mainly of fish and small aquatic invertebrates.

Mallard hen

Painting: "Alaska Mallards"

Mallard drake

The mallard is one of the most common and widespread ducks in North America. Its vivid colors and large size makes it a favorite amongst bird watchers and hunters.

Mallard

Mallard ducklings

Ducks are divided into two groups. The dabbling or puddle ducks inhabit shallow waters and feed by "tipping up". These ducks include mallards, pintails, wigeon and teal. The diving ducks inhabit deeper waters and feed by diving into the depths. These ducks include eider, redheads, scaups, canvasbacks and goldeneyes. Puddle ducks take flight by jumping straight up while diving ducks usually have to run across the water surface before taking flight.

Mallards

Pintail hen

Pintail drake

Hooded Merganser hen

The Northern pintail is another of North America's more common ducks. The males have a brown head, white neck and underparts, and a long, black tail. The female is brownish with a somewhat pointed tail. Nests in marshes, ponds, and on tundra. Males have a distinct whistle call and the females quack.

Alaska is a prime habitat for waterfowl nesting. Here, the long summer hours provide ample food for the growing families. Above, a large flock of pintails feed in a field near Fairbanks before separating and seeking individual nesting sites further north.

Although somewhat rare in Alaska, the colorful Redhead duck is a sought-after quarry for bird watchers hereabouts. The male's brick-red head and black breast make it an easy specie to identify. It has a very unusual "meow-like" call. Its numbers have greatly declined over the years due to both hunting and habitat destruction.

The American wigeon (male) sports a green ear patch, white crown and a brownish body. Its bill is a pale blue and it is a "dabbling" duck. The brownish female lines her nest in down and locates it inland from the waters edge to help minimize its detection by predators that often patrol the shorelines.

The Great Blue heron is found along waterways in the more southern parts of Alaska. This tall fish-eating bird stands 4 feet high and has a 6 foot wingspan. It can often be seen standing motionless in shallow water until dispatching its prey with a quick stab.

MAMMALS
OF
ALASKA

"Mountain Monarchs"

MAMMALS

Alaska's mammals range from the King of the Arctic (Polar bear) down to the tiny, ferocious shrew. Animals such as Dall sheep, Beluga whales, muskoxen, caribou, and Arctic fox join the Polar bear as being somewhat unique to Alaska and the northcountry. Other animals such as Black bears, goats, elk, coyotes, fox, wolves and moose are mammals that inhabit Alaska but are also found in many of America's other states. It is this extensive and varied array of wildlife that makes Alaska truly "a place like no other".

The following section is of the "Mammals of Alaska". It is a portfolio of many of Alaska's favorite and/or familiar mammals. Maps illustrate the locations of many of the species.

A trio of wolves (from a pack of eight) pauses from their play to focus on a nearby howling wolf. Soon the whole pack joined in song.

Author's Journal *(Sept. 9, '72, Mankomen Lake)*
Spent the last two days camped out on a bluff overlooking a wolf den near
my winter's cabin. Counted 13 different wolves, all in various shades of gray.

The DALL SHEEP in Alaska

Dall sheep (Ovis dalli dalli) inhabit the rugged, high peaks of Alaska's mountains. The white sheep has a coat to match the snow, and in spring and summer, against dark cliffs or green mountain meadows, can be seen from miles away.

Older Dall rams have massive, flaring, amber-colored horns, while ewes and young rams have slender, shorter horns. Horns continue to grow throughout the life of the animal, unlike antlers which are shed and regrown annually.

Although wolves are the main natural predator of Dall sheep, weather is the most important determinate of populations, as bad weather can cut off needed food supplies.

Author's Journal *(Jan. 15, '82, Fairbanks)*

Just read that severe wind conditions apparently killed as much as one-fifth of the Dall sheep in many areas of the Alaska Range. Deep snow with icy crust and a late spring snow both were prime causes of the decline. Adults and lambs were victims.

**Note: Dall sheep are also referred to as Dall's sheep.

Mature Dall rams weigh up to 275 pounds and stand 3 feet high. Ewes seldom weigh over 140 pounds.

Dall rams often sport signs of battles and/or falls. Broken horns, noses, etc., are common on older animals.

Dall ram (winter coat)

Horn Study

A "full curl" takes 7-10 years to grow. Also, the tips of horns are often "broomed" (broken off).

The mating season occurs in November/December. Horn-clashing fights break out amongst the rams to determine who will mate with the ewes. The majority of serious fighting is reserved for males who are similar in horn-size and hence must fight to determine dominance. Smaller horned rams normally do not challenge the large rams.

Dall rams (summer coat)

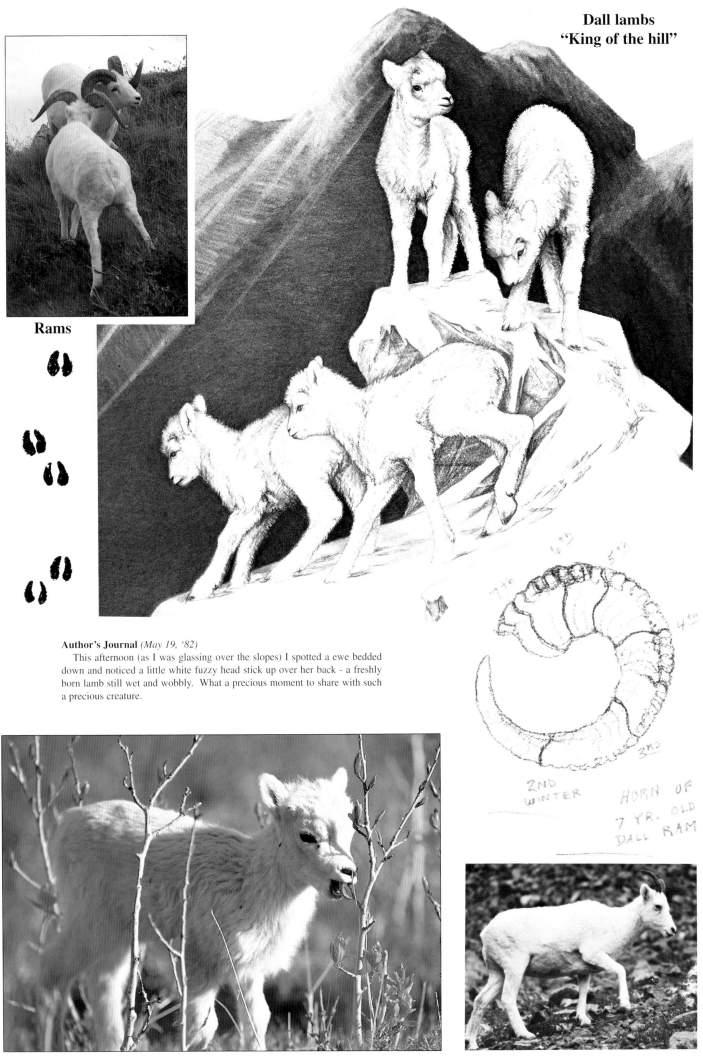

Dall lambs
"King of the hill"

Rams

Author's Journal *(May 19, '82)*

This afternoon (as I was glassing over the slopes) I spotted a ewe bedded down and noticed a little white fuzzy head stick up over her back - a freshly born lamb still wet and wobbly. What a precious moment to share with such a precious creature.

7TH
6TH
5TH
4TH
3RD
2ND WINTER

HORN OF 7 YR. OLD DALL RAM

Dall lamb browsing on springtime vegetation.

Ewe

Dall sheep

Ram tracks

Ewe with nursing lamb / June

These fighting matches are impressive and the clashing of their horns can be heard a mile away. During these fights, the two rams will rise up on their hind feet and then drop to all fours and charge one another from 5-10 yards. A bone-jarring "Clak" follows, rendering them stunned and motionless for a few moments before they separate to begin anew.

These two "unmatched" rams spent the day gently butting horns but not fighting seriously as those in the above photo were.

**Old ram
"broomed horn"**

Author's Journal *(July 13, '77, Denali Nat'l Park)*
   Went up Igloo Mountain yesterday and came up the backside and across the mountains of Sable Pass today. Counted 97 sheep total on both these slopes. One Sable Pass flock numbered 43 ewes and lambs.

Nursing lamb / June

Ram

Ewe and lamb / June

Newborn Dall lambs survey the first human they have probably ever seen. Born in late May/early June, they are able to run and keep up with their mothers within a day or so, thereby making them safe from most predators.

A large autumn ram. Dall sheep seldom live beyond 12 or 13 years in the wild.

The MOUNTAIN GOAT
in Alaska

Range of the Mountain Goat
in Alaska
(shaded area)

Nannies

Of all of Alaska's large mammals, none lives in terrain more dangerous than that occupied by the Mountain goat. Avalanches and rock slides are normal occurences in this rocky, steep environment.

The Alaskan Mountain goat is a resident of rugged, mountain terrain. Its all-white coat and short horns cause it to be often confused with its high country neighbor, the Dall sheep, especially the ewes. The males (or billies) and females (nannies) are very similar in appearance, both having horns also. 200/300 pound adults is normal.

A single "kid" is born to the nannies in May/June, following the November/December mating of the adults. While the males tend to keep to themselves or with a few other males, the females and young tend to herd up together. Herds of 100 or more are not uncommon in prime terrain.

Perhaps because they live in such inaccessible country and therefore seem to have few enemies, they are not as wary as most big game animals. They do, however, occasionally cross valleys when seeking mineral "licks" or changing ranges and are very vulnerable to predators when in the low country. Although their sharp horns provide able weapons for defense, they are usually unable to match the deadly killing ability of wolves and bears, and the young goats (especially) make easy prey. Alaska's Mountain goats may live to 15 years.

Goat hair is a source of the famous Chilkat blankets weaved by the Tlingit Indian women of southeastern Alaska.

Nannie and kid

Billy

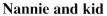

Immature billy

Billy

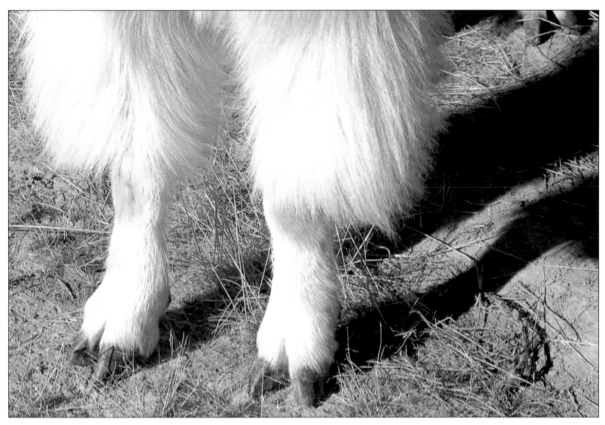

The Mountain goat has hooves that allow it to traverse the sharp, rocky heights of Alaska's mountains. Its dense white coat also helps it conserve heat during the long, frigid winters.

Weather and accidents are the main sources of mortality amongst Mountain goats. Few predators would brave this hazardous terrain to pursue them.

Mountain Goat track

Author's Journal *(Nov. 26, 2001, Haines, AK.)*

Spent a few days with the Bald eagles who have migrated into the area to feed on the late run of salmon. Very, very cold and only a few hundred eagles are still here. Friends told me the peak (a few thousand eagles) was about ten days ago. Found a few goats in the high country but everytime I managed to get within camera range they spooked higher. Too dangerous to pursue.

Adult 48" TALL

Walking tracks

3"

Billy & Kid
September 2001

Hooves, horns, eyes & nose are black

A "billy" Mountain goat eyes the photographer in the above September photo. His horns are usually heavier in appearance than those of the females, but not necessarily longer.

112

Antlers (in "velvet")

Horns

Antlers or Horns?: The main difference between the two is that antlers are grown and shed every year and horns are never shed and grow longer with age. Also, antlers are made of bone while horns are made of keratin (similar to our fingernails).

The horns of goats and sheep will also indicate the animals' age. A series of lines (like the rings in a tree) around the horn will separate one year's growth from the next.

Kid (autumn)

Kids, usually born on a mountain ledge, can stand and climb shortly after their May/June birth.

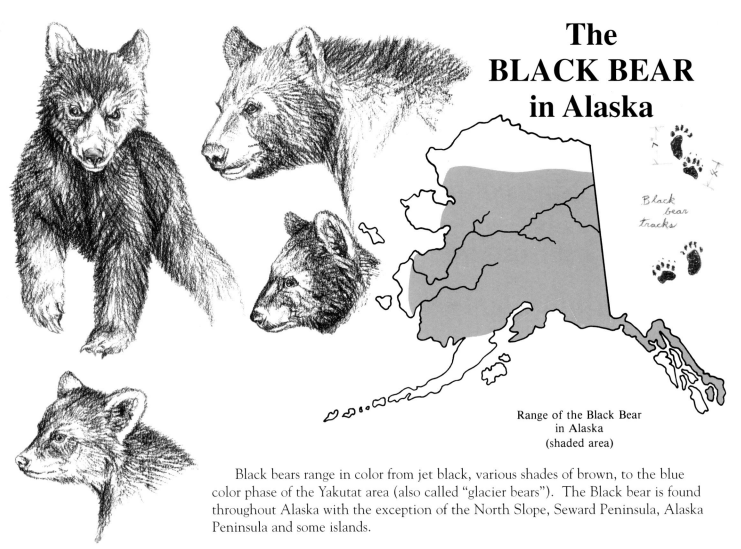

The BLACK BEAR in Alaska

Black bear tracks

Range of the Black Bear
in Alaska
(shaded area)

Black bears range in color from jet black, various shades of brown, to the blue color phase of the Yakutat area (also called "glacier bears"). The Black bear is found throughout Alaska with the exception of the North Slope, Seward Peninsula, Alaska Peninsula and some islands.

Black bear: Alaska population is over 50,000.

Black bear/brown phase

Young cubs spend much of their time playing or exploring. Their first months are spent either close to mother's side or up in trees if danger appears. Black coats are the commonest color of Alaska's Black bears.

At birth the Black bear weighs about 6 ounces and is blind and hairless. They emerge in the spring from their den weighing about 5 pounds.

An average adult Black bear weighs about 180 pounds and measures about five feet from nose to tail. They do not have the distinctive shoulder hump the grizzly does and have a straight facial profile as compared to the grizzlies' "dished" forehead. Their claws are sharply curved and seldom over 1-1/2 inches long, making them perfect for the tree climbing they do throughout their life.

Blacks mate in June or July. At most other times of year they are solitary animals. Cubs, usually two, are born the following February. The cubs usually den with their mother for the first winter following birth after which they are driven off to fend for themselves.

After emerging from their winter den, the Black bears seek out freshly sprouted green vegetation. As summer progresses, the bears seek out the salmon runs as well as the emerging berry crop. An occasional moose calf or carrion-find helps sustain them through the year and helps them enter their den with a full belly and enough fat for their body to live on through their long winter sleep.

Black bears are plentiful here in Alaska and bear/human encounters are common, especially when human garbage is carelessly or improperly disposed of. The bears are routinely seen even in Alaska's largest cities. Caution must always be exercised when encountering these bears. Normally the bears will flee when encountered, but they have been known to stalk and kill humans upon occasion.

Black bear boar

Bears and wolves are predators that have frequent interaction. Sometimes a large or aggressive bear can drive wolves from their kill, but usually it is the wolf pack that will harass a bear until it reluctantly relinquishes its kill or carrion find.

Bear attack: If attacked by a Brown/Grizzly bear, experts usually suggest that a person fall to the ground (belly down with hands behind your neck) and play dead. If a smaller Black bear attacks, however, and continues to bite you as you lay still, it is likely a predatory attack and one should fight and kick aggressively at the bear.

Black bears have exceptional smell and can often detect carrion or prey from miles away. Their eyesight and hearing are comparable to that of humans.

Bears that wake early from hibernation are often able to smell and then dig out marmots that are still sleeping in their winter dens.

The
BROWN BEAR / GRIZZLY
in Alaska

Range of Brown Bear
in Alaska
(shaded area)

Alaska often has multiple bear-people conflicts annually. About 20 people have died throughout Alaska during the past 80 years from bear attacks. From 1970-1996, incidentally, 2,300 bears were killed by people in "self-defense".

It is estimated that about 80 Black bears and 4 or 5 Brown bears occupy the low country between south Anchorage and Eagle River. Also, about 250 Black bears and 60 Brown bears roam throughout the whole Anchorage municipality.

Perhaps no predator in North America is as aggressive or efficient at killing prey as a Brown/Grizzly. Although their primary diet is berries, roots and fish, they will fearlessly attack large, formidable mammals such as moose and muskoxen.

Brown / Grizzly bear: Alaska population is 35,000 to 50,000.

Grizzly cubs have very individual personalities. Some seem playful and curious, while others seem either timid or very aggressive and domineering. Some never seem to leave mother's side, while others will occasionally stray until called back by a scolding mother.

Male bears will sometimes kill young cubs in order to induce the female to again desire to breed.

Grizzlies

Wildlife photography is a popular pastime of Alaskans and tourists. Here a sow grizzly and cubs came out of the brush and scattered a group of hikers in Denali National Park. The running people were chased by the bears until they reached my vehicle, an indication that running often incites the "chase instinct" of predatory animals.

120

The grizzly is now making his final stand in the Far North, having been gradually and relentlessly pushed ever deeper into the remote and inaccessible regions of western North America by the spreading masses of people. It is now a threatened species south of the Canadian border. The grizzly and Brown bear are now considered a single specie: Ursus arctos.

Awesomely respected for his courage, strength and ferocity, it is given a wide berth by other creatures. Fiercely aggressive when wounded, cornered or defending its young, the grizzly can quickly and efficiently dispose of any opponent foolish enough to challenge him.

The grizzly somewhat resembles its close relative, the Black bear. The grizzly, however, is usually larger (an adult male can weigh as much as 1,400 pounds), has a more prominent shoulder hump, longer and straighter claws, and a broader, dished face. Both species have a wide range of color phases.

The grizzly is omnivorous; that is, it feeds on both vegetable and animal substances. The bear is not considered a significant predator on big game species, except those old, injured or newly-born.

During winter the bears seek out sheltered dens to "hibernate" in. The young, hairless and weighing less than a pound, are born in the sow's winter den. Two cubs are the usual litter.

Bears have an uncanny sense of their home location. Troublesome bears have been transplanted hundreds of miles away, only to return "home" within a few weeks. That is why a "fed bear is often a dead bear". Humans that are careless with their garbage, pet foods, etc., have to take the responsibility if bears become accustomed to these food sources and are thereafter destroyed.

"Don't Mess With Mom"

Sow

Study

Blueberries

Grizzlies / springtime play

Sow

Boars and sows usually live apart except during summer mating season and when reluctantly sharing a stretch of river to fish salmon.

Autumn is a time of changing leaves, ripening berries, and salmon runs. It is the season when bears must fatten up in order to have the reserves needed to survive their long winter's hibernation.

Author's Journal *(Aug. 27, '74, Anchorage area)*
Just read in the paper that a man was killed and eaten by a Brown bear down at Cold Bay. These stories always make me pause in my tracks for a little "reflecting" on my chosen profession.
A person being killed by a bear isn't particularly a novel event hereabouts; but a person being eaten by a bear is still, thankfully, fairly rare.

A Pink salmon thrashes its way through the shallows enroute to its spawning grounds. It is here that they are most vulnerable to bears, eagles, and other predators.

Author's Journal *(Oct. 17, '71, Mankomen Lake)*

Two grizzlies left their tracks on the trail in back of the cabin last night. I "glassed" three caribou swimming across the lake as I stood on the beach at the west end of the lake this afternoon. They beached about a hundred yards west of the cabin, shook, and disappeared into the brush.

Tonight, a beautiful night. No big-city or civilization noises to distract from the sounds and sights of nature. No sirens or TV to drown out the whisperings of the wind; no glaring lights or tall buildings to rob ones sight of the moon, slowly drifting above snow-smothered mountains. And to breath the crisp, wild air is to know you are really alive. Tonight, God, the feeling of my freedom is a silent conversation between You and I. Here I can feel the power of Your hand: the mountains, the stars, the very air. Here then is my cathedral. Here then I believe. In the city, amongst man and his puny sculptures of concrete, of metal and glass, I sometimes lose sight of the magnificent mountains or forget to watch the lazy moon cross the sky. It is then that I sometimes lose sight of You.

Author's Journal *(Sept. 13, '78, Kenai Peninsula)*

A sow grizzly with two yearling cubs gave me quite a start today. I came up a hill from one side and the three of them came up the hill from the other side. We met at the top. It is times such as these that one longs hungrily for his absent .338 Winchester Magnum! One of the cubs paused before finally deciding to follow the fleeing sow and cub back down the hill. At the bottom of the hill they stopped. The sow and one cub stood on their hind legs and looked around before continuing on.

Why does a grizzly chase a herd of uncatchable sheep across a mountain meadow but yet flees in seeming terror from one unarmed, very catchable man? (I'm not "complaining" mind you!)

Hibernation: In Alaska, bears may spend 5-7 months in their winter den. This seems to be necessary for a bears survival as food is often scarce or unavailable during this time. A bears body temperature and metabolic rate is reduced during this "sleep" and hence the bear is able to live off its body reserves until it is able to again feed. Occasionally, and seemingly without any purpose, the bears may emerge from their dens during winter for a short period. Boars (males) normally enter their dens later than pregnant sows (females) and also emerge earlier.

Alaska, incidentally, contains about 98 percent of the United States population of Brown/Grizzly bears.

Grizzly claws are much straighter and longer than those of the Black bear.

The POLAR BEAR in Alaska

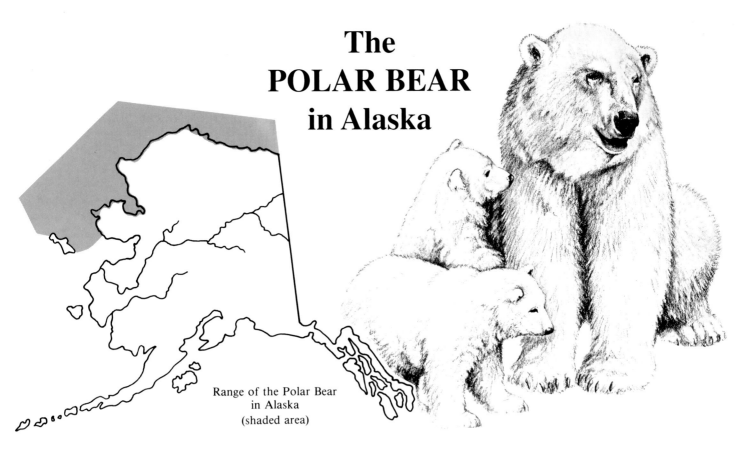

Range of the Polar Bear
in Alaska
(shaded area)

Polar bears are most abundant near Alaska's northern coastline and the southern edge of the ice.

Cub

The Polar bear (Ursus maritimus), is Alaska's most mysterious bear and lives at the edge of the arctic ice. The summer months find the bears usually ranging between 71 and 72 degrees north latitude. There is a limited amount of denning activity on Alaska's north coast. The Polar bear, like most creatures of this harsh environment, is an animal well suited to his surroundings.

Its coloring is white with a slight tinge of yellow. The color matches its environment and often the only thing visible against the snowy ice-covered arctic background is his black nose and dark eyes. Little wonder they can sneak up so near their prey (usually seals) without being detected. The Polar bear also feeds on carrion (mostly whale and walrus) that it finds washed up along the coast.

Polar and Brown bears both evolved from a common ancestor and have similar weights. Large males of both species can weigh up to 1,400 pounds, but 600 to 1,200 is average. Females take to their winter dens in late October and the cubs are born in December; remaining with their mother until they are about 28 months old. They are then "disowned" by the female and she once again roams the icepack alone until the urge to mate again drives her to seek male companionship. Males remain with and breed a female for only a short time before seeking out other females to breed.

Human hunters are the Polar bear's only real predator besides the packs of killer whales that also hunt the arctic waters.

These cubs were taken into captivity after they lost their mothers.

Polar bears seldom venture far inland from the coast. Occasionally, however, weather and ice conditions will force the bears to remain ashore for long periods without food. It is then that they often come into conflict with humans. Churchill, Manitoba is a prime example of Polar bear and human interaction.

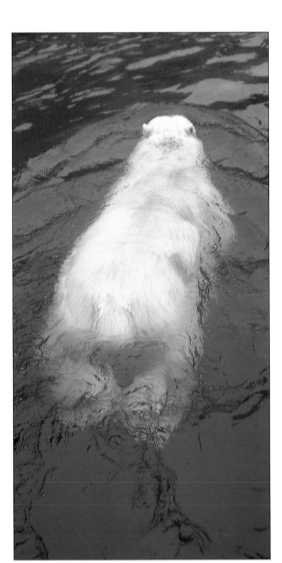

Cub

Polar bears have hollow hairs which allow them to remain warm and afloat in the chilled arctic waters. Bears are sometimes seen miles from the nearest land or ice formation.

Cub / April

Sow

Alaska's Polar bears and Brown bears look and exist quite differently. But, interestingly, the Polar bear is actually just a changed Brown bear that evolved during the last Ice Age.

Ringed seals are the Polar bear's main prey. Two hunting techniques are employed: ambushing the seals at their breathing holes, and sneaking up on sleeping seals.

Arctic foxes are commonly seen following the "King of the Ice" and feeding on leftover scraps.

©2002 1010 LINDSTRAND

"Peaceful Arctic"

Arctic fox

Cubs

Polar bear: Alaska population is 4,000 to 6,000.

Twin cubs are the commonest litter. They emerge from their winter's den in March/April weighing about 15 pounds. Cubs stay with their mother until they are about 28 months old.

Siblings often roam the icepack together until they reach breeding age. They then separate to seek mates but will often recognize and play with one another if they should cross paths later.

The SITKA BLACK-TAILED DEER in Alaska

"Spike" buck

Winter is a time of scarcity for Alaska's animals and long hours must be spent searching for adequate food.

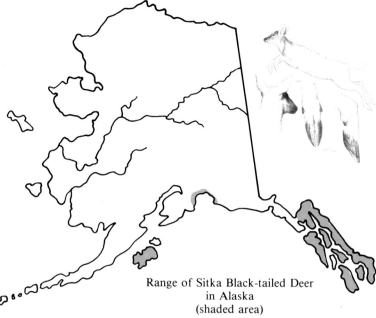

Range of Sitka Black-tailed Deer in Alaska (shaded area)

The Sitka Black-tailed deer (Odocoileus hemionus sitkensis) is a much smaller, stockier deer than other black-tails. A mature buck (male) averages 120-140 pounds, while the adult doe will weigh 80-90 pounds. The buck's antlers are small with a typical black-tail formation.

Fawn / June

The breeding season usually peaks in November, with the spotted fawns being born in May / June. A normal life span is 10-12 years.

A young buck in early autumn. Its oddly-shaped antlers may indicate that they were injured during formation.

Study

Deer populations fluctuate greatly in Alaska due to the severity of winters and predation. Clearcut logging can also deprive the deer herds of necessary winter range and shelter.

Mature does begin breeding in their second year and will normally bear two fawns annually during their prime years.

Top: Buck in July "velvet". **Bottom:** Spike buck "challenging" another small buck to a friendly sparring match.

Buck & fawn

June
SE Alaska

2 lines of spots
run down back →

The "fuzzy velvet" contains blood vessels which feed the growing antlers beneath. When the antlers reach full growth (August / September) the velvet is shed.

Fawns are able to stand and run within hours of birth. During their first few weeks, however, the still fragile fawns will spend a lot of time hiding from potential predators and sleeping.

The ROOSEVELT ELK in Alaska

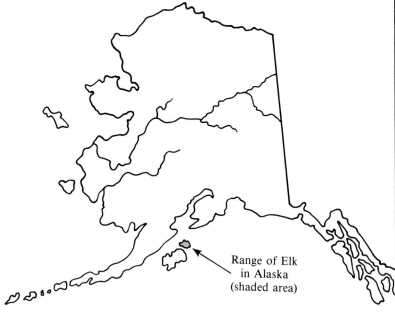

Range of Elk in Alaska (shaded area)

Bulls (August)

Roosevelt elk (Cervus canadenis roosevelti) found in Alaska are the result of a transplant of eight elk from the state of Washington in 1928. At present, elk are only found on a few of the smaller islands of Alaska.

Bull (September)

Roosevelt elk are darker in color, larger, and have more massive antlers than do the Rocky Mountain elk. A large bull from Alaska will often weigh over 1,200 pounds and sport long, sweeping antlers.

Elk are distinguished by their dark legs and neck, yellowish rump and large brown bodies. Cows, unlike caribou cows, do not grow antlers. Calves are born in May/June and, like deer, have spotted coats for protective camouflage.

In September the annual "rut" begins. It is during this period that the eerie "bugling" of the area's bulls are heard. By late October the mating has been completed and the bands of elk migrate to lower wintering grounds.

A large bull elk in early antler growth. From this stage the velvet-covered antlers will continue to grow throughout the summer until the antlers have matured. They then shed the velvet (above, opposite page) and with polished antlers (below, opposite page) they prepare for the season's "rut" where they must fight other bulls in their attempt to gain dominance and thereby the right to breed the harem of cows.

Roosevelt Elk
Study

5 ft. beams
6 points = mature
bull

5 ft. tall

Bugling
Sept.

Cow/July
450-600 pds.

Alaska elk antlers have a
tendency towards "crowning"; the
formation of 3 points at the end
of each antler.

Swelled neck during "rut"

Roosevelt elk bulls
have shorter but more massive
antlers than Rocky Mountain elk bulls.
September study / 2001

BULL WALKING

Calf / autumn

138

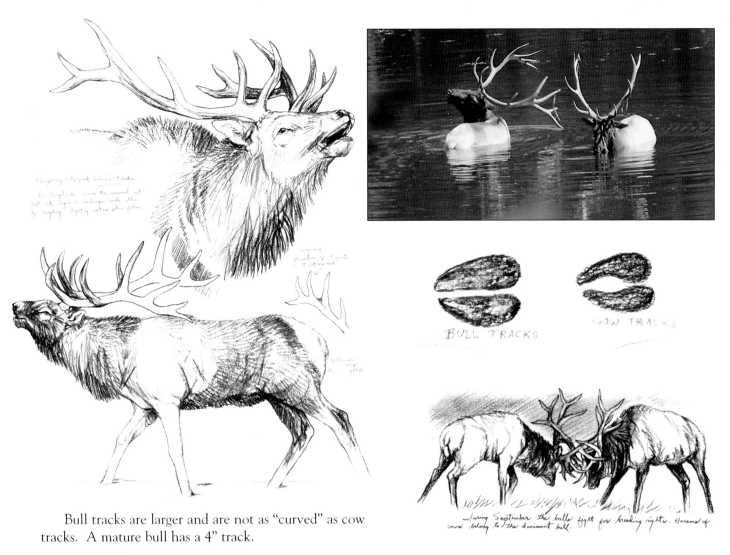

Bull tracks are larger and are not as "curved" as cow tracks. A mature bull has a 4" track.

A calf in July. The calves tend to band together until their mothers return from their feeding to nurse them. They often lie motionless in cover until they hear their mothers call; hence helping them be protected from prowling predators such as bears.

The CARIBOU in Alaska

Caribou bull

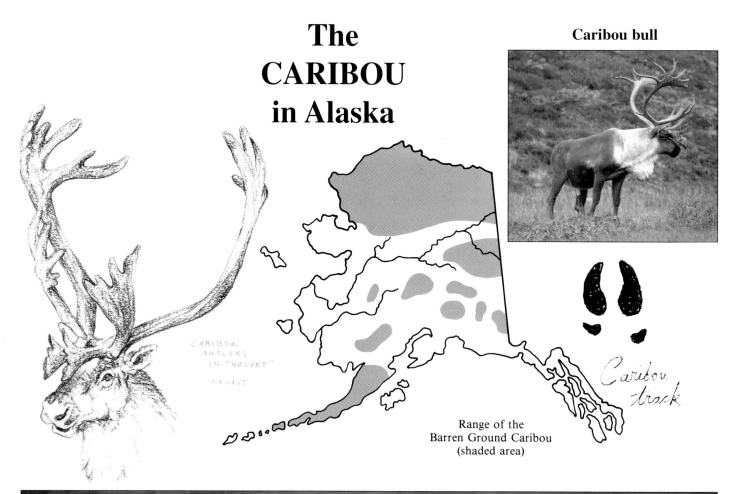

CARIBOU ANTLERS IN "VELVET"

AUGUST

Range of the
Barren Ground Caribou
(shaded area)

Caribou track

Caribou are known as "wanderers of the north", a trait necessary to keep them from overgrazing the available food supply.

A pair of caribou bulls graze in Denali National Park.

The Barren-ground caribou (Rangifer tarandus) is a large, stout deer that is generally associated with the arctic tundra of North America. The specie is a resident throughout much of Alaska, with the exception of the Southeastern panhandle and most offshore islands. It has been estimated that there are approximately 900,000 wild caribou in Alaska today. Both sexes grow antlers and an adult bull can weigh 400 pounds to the cows 200 pounds.

Caribou are nomadic animals who must continuously keep migrating in order to find adequate food. This prevents overgrazing by the herds, thus preventing starvation scenes that are not uncommon amongst other deer family members. Because they occasionally change migration routes, the Native hunters who have come to rely on them are sometimes deprived of this valuable source of food and clothing.

Caribou bulls "rut" in September/October and the cows calve in May/June, shortly after arriving at their traditional "calving grounds". The single calf is able to walk within an hour of birth.

**Antlers
in
"velvet"**

Spring coat

141

A large bull caribou in late September. He has just recently shed his velvet; leaving his antlers stained in blood.

Cow caribou shed their antlers later than bulls and normally don't shed them until after their calves are born in the spring. Antlers are rich in calcium and other minerals, and when they are shed the squirrels, lemmings, porcupines and other northern animals chew on them. Most shed antlers are therefore "recycled" within a year or two.

Author's Journal *(Sept. 4, '81, Denali area)*
Sat and watched three nice caribou bulls today. Impressive creatures with their tall, wide antlers and full autumn colors. They aren't fighting amongst one another and are still eating - meaning that the "rut" is not yet on.

Author's Journal *(Aug. 17, '74, Mt. McKinley, Alaska)*
Today I witnessed one of Nature's tales unfold. Today I watched a pack of wolves run down and kill a caribou.

Last night I pitched my sleeping bag in the Wyoming Hills east of the Toklat River. It was a clear night so I didn't bother with a tent. While munching my way through a couple of apples and some beef jerky, I listened to a pack of wolves a'howling down on the river flats. A little later, in fading light, I glassed a pair of wolves trotting across the flats. They paused atop a tiny knoll to howl once. Moments later their howl was answered with howls from further up the flats. There were caribou passing through these foothills and the wolves were hungry.

This morning as I moved upriver, I could see that the flats had been busy. Caribou and wolf tracks were everywhere. The wolves were still hunting.

Then, early this afternoon, I climbed out of the river flats to glass the area upriver. As soon as I got myself up high enough, I sat down and looked over the country. It was then that I saw the kill.

A pack of 6 wolves were nipping and lunging at a cow caribou, who paused and turned and flailed her front legs and shook her tiny antlers at the circling pack. Then she broke from the pack and ran, soon putting some yardage between her and the pack. She was hurt, bleeding, but she wasn't a quitter, she wanted to live.

And then, all at once, her will to live seemed to leave her. She stopped a third of the way up a gentle slope, and with her head hung she waited for her executioners. One wolf hit her at the throat and the rest dug their teeth in somewhere and pulled her down. Wihin seconds the wolves were feeding.

A half mile further up the valley a young caribou looked back. It was now an orphan.

Caribou bull (summer coat)

Reindeer cow

A few small shipments of reindeer were imported into Alaska from Siberia in the late 1800's to help sustain the northern Eskimos when the caribou herds altered their normal migration routes. The caribou and reindeer share the same scientific name and can interbreed, often to the detriment of the caribou.

142

Author's Journal *(Nov. 14, '71, Mankomen Lake)*

   Hundreds and hundreds and hundreds of caribou moving through the area. Very unusual to look out the cabin window and not see some migrating by during these past few days.

   A mature bull caribou in late August. His antlers have about matured in size and soon he will begin to shed the "velvet" that has nourished their growth throughout the spring and summer months. Bulls usually drop their antlers by December.

By September the bulls have acquired their magnificent autumn coats and, with polished antlers, begin to fight other bulls for the rights to mate with the area's cows.

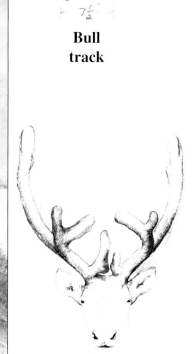

Bull track

"Autumn Splendor"

A caribou's antlers usually reach a maximum size during their sixth year.

Caribou bull

The caribou's main food are the lichens that cover the Arctic tundra. During summer months their diet also includes willows and other vegetation.

The MOOSE in Alaska

Range of Moose
in Alaska
(shaded area)

Alaskan bull moose

Shedding "velvet"

The Alaskan moose (Alces alces) is the largest moose in the world and ranges throughout most of the state from the panhandle of Southeast to the Arctic slope. A member of the deer family and somewhat ridiculously-looking, the moose is nevertheless a majestic, well suited wilderness creature. It is perhaps the most commonly seen big game animal in the state.

A bull in prime condition may weigh upwards of 1,500 pounds (an adult cow about 3/4 as much) and many Alaskans depend almost entirely upon moose for their year-round meat supply. Antlers, shed annually, can spread up to 80 inches and weigh 60-plus pounds.

Moose breed in the autumn with the peak of "rut" activities in September/October. It is during this season that the huge bulls are most often hunted, for they are not especially wary at this time (their breeding instinct overpowers their usual sense of caution) and will come readily to the call of a hunter's birchbark horn. Fearless rutting bulls have no hesitation about "charging", even oncoming train locomotives!

As winter progresses and food sources become scarcer, the moose band into herds. When the herd has exhausted the food supply in one area, their long legs will carry them through the deepest snowdrifts to new locations to browse on the twigs and bark of willows, birch, and alders, until that, too, becomes exhausted. Hard winters take a heavy toll of moose, either through starvation, disease, or by falling prey to the deadly wolf packs.

In mid-winter the antlers drop from the heads of the bulls and the cows become heavy with calves. Calves are born in May or June, one or two being the usual number, and stay with their mother for 12 months or until she again approaches giving birth. The cow then forcibly ejects her last-year's "400 pound babies" from her side and leaves them to their own self-sufficiency.

The bull moose that are not able to become dominant will often spend time "practice fighting" with other bulls. These matches are seldom serious; mainly pushing and rattling. One bull is "collared".

Moose are commonly seen in towns throughout Alaska feeding on trees, plants and gardens.

Author's Journal *(Aug. 29, '83)*

Photographed two big bull moose up a draw near Sanctuary River early this morning. Sat down and watched them as they browsed and bedded down. The moose have been getting aggressive these last few days. Don't dare get too close or they'll charge and they're beginning to clash antlers together.

At times a bull will thrash a small tree until it's shreds!

Bull / autumn

Subsistence and recreational hunters are often at odds with the tourists and residents that want only to view wildlife. Wolves and bears are major predators, and Alaska Department of Fish & Game has estimated that in the Nelchina basin (as an example) about 500 wolves and 1,500 bears killed between 9,000 and 12,000 moose in 1998/1999. The hunters want the predator numbers greatly reduced in order to increase the moose and caribou populations. The "viewers", however, want nature to balance the prey/predator numbers without human intervention.

Bull / spring

This bull came down to the marsh to drink and to also lick and nibble on the moist soil to, conceivably, obtain needed minerals.

A bull moose rests amongst the autumn colored foliage of central Alaska.

"Call to Battle"

Bull moose in "velvet" / August

Moose often feed on submerged vegetation. This food is high in nutrition, and a large bull can eat up to 50 pounds daily. Moose can remain completely submerged for long periods, and only raise their head to breathe, chew, and scan the surroundings for danger. Also, moose sometimes head to shallow water if pursued by bears or wolves. Their long legs will give them an advantage there.

Cow moose and calves / June

Author's Journal *(Dec. 19, '74, Matanuska Valley)*

A herd of 32 moose were browsing out on the flats bordering the Matanuska River north of Eagle River this morning. It was the biggest "herding" of moose I had ever seen here in Alaska, looking almost like a Minnesota dairy farm from a distance. The previous largest herd was 24, which I saw back in 1971, bedded down in "downtown" North Pole.

Moose will often herd up when the snow gets high or when there are a lot of wolves in the area. Herding up offers some protection from predators (as there are often "very aggressive" individuals found within a herd, which often act as sort of the herd's "protectors" and which will often protect the weaker moose from attack) and also it provides more "legs" to break trail through the deep snow to various feeding yards. A lone moose would soon grow weak if he had to break all the trails himself.

Monday I will drive back down to the Matanuska River and see if I can find this herd again. I had my camera with me this morning, but alas, no skis. Without skis (or snowshoes) I wouldn't have gotten two feet off the road before going "under".

Author's Journal *(Dec. 8, 2001, Homer)*

Cold weather and new snow equals some beautiful winter landscapes. Snowshoed around the hills taking pictures. A number of moose have moved into downtown to feast on the trees and shrubs. Followed a scavenging Red fox along the ocean beach for a few hours before losing him in the driftwood snags.

Bull / December

In Alaska, about 700 moose are killed yearly by vehicles and another 100 are killed by trains. The meat can often be salvaged by residents and charities.

Bull moose in mid-August.

Cow nursing twin calves. Cow moose are extremely protective and prove to be formidable foes when they or their calves are threatened by predators such as wolves and bears.

The antlers of exceptional bulls can spread 80" and weigh over 60 pounds.

Cow

Cow moose in their prime usually give birth to twin calves. The cow (above) was photographed in early June north of Talkeetna, Alaska. Her rare "triplets" occur about once in a few thousand moose births.

The MUSKOX in Alaska

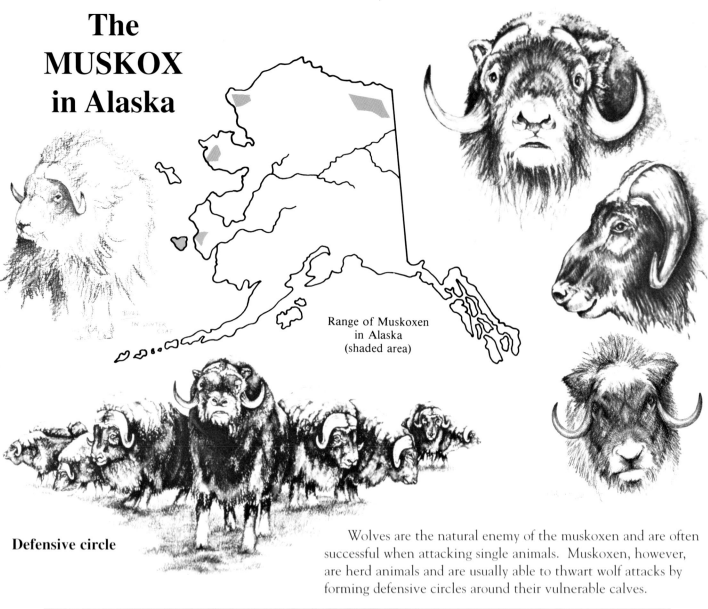

Range of Muskoxen
in Alaska
(shaded area)

Defensive circle

Wolves are the natural enemy of the muskoxen and are often successful when attacking single animals. Muskoxen, however, are herd animals and are usually able to thwart wolf attacks by forming defensive circles around their vulnerable calves.

Bull. Oomingmok is an Eskimo word for muskoxen.

The muskoxen (Ovibos moschatus) is a creature well suited to live in its harsh environment. A mature bull averages 600-800 pounds, while the smaller cows weigh 400-500 pounds. A coat of long warm hair, cloven hooves, and a shoulder hump, further distinguishes this arctic dweller. Both sexes grow horns.

Calf / May   **Bull / September**

Muskox tracks

During summer months, the muskoxen sheds its wool-like underhair called "qiviut". This is one of the world's rarest fibers, and Alaska Natives often gather it to make warm garments such as hats and scarves.

Author's Journal *(Sept. 23, '01, Tok, Alaska)*
   Recently, up north, an observer witnessed a grizzly kill four muskoxen. He commented that the bear was extremely methodical and was able to single the prey out and kill them individually.
   Wolves (especially packs), if patient and methodical, are also able to occasionally pick off lone muskoxen and unprotected calves.

An immature bull muskoxen (photo). It is estimated that about 2,000 muskoxen now live in Alaska. A limited-permit hunt is now allowed in some areas of the state. Herds are found scattered along the northern coast of Alaska as well as on Nunivak Island. The University of Alaska/Fairbanks offers tours of their muskox research farm; enabling those unable to reach the remote wild herds a close-up view of these fascinating northern animals.

A cow and calf warily eye the intruding photographer. Single calves are born from April to June and normally weigh between 20-30 pounds.

A bull muskoxen skull. Four or five inches of heavy horn "bosses" help protect the bulls during their aggressive head-smashing of the annual rut. The "crack" of this impact can be heard a mile away.

The BISON in Alaska

Range of Bison
in Alaska
(shaded area)

Calves are born a reddish brown and are able to stand and nurse within an hour or so. Born from April to August in Alaska, the calves begin browsing and grazing within a week of their birth. The calf below is approximately one week old and spends much of his day running and jumping with other herd calves.

Bison usually move along under the leadership of an older cow. Once or twice a day they will seek out a watering source and can often be seen rolling around in mud and dust to discourage the ever present insects.

Calf

Bull / January

Alaska's bison herds of today all originated from a 1928 transplant of 20 cows and bulls from Montana.. Today they have been spread to various locations throughout the state and their numbers have grown substantially, enough to allow selected hunting in some areas.

The Alaskan bison (Bison bison) is a large, formidable and adaptable mammal. Bulls stand 6 feet high at the shoulder and weigh in at over a ton; cows weigh about 2/3's of that. Huge back humps and large heads with upward curving horns further distinguish the animal. Wild bison have been known to live over 20 years, a rarity amongst Alaska's hoofed animals.

Bison have been known to inflict huge damage on Alaska's fledgling agricultural industry, especially in the Delta Junction area of the state. Migratory animals, the herds often leave their spring calving grounds to move into the more human-populated areas for the harsher winters. Often they arrive before the farmer's crops are harvested, causing problems, problems that have at times been settled with guns. Bison, somewhat like elephants, are hard to discourage when they desire to feed on a crop. Because of their strength and huge size, a "mere" fence is often no deterrent.

The bison was Alaska's most common large land mammal thousands of years ago before it was brought to extinction in the state.

A weeks old calf nurses from its mother in the warm spring sun. The rich milk will sustain the calf until it is old enough to browse and graze. Its orangish/reddish coat will darken in a few months.

Young bull bison kicking up the dust and sparring during early autumn.

Left: A yearling bull. It has now been "disowned" by its mother who has recently given birth to a new calf.
Right: Adult cow. Both cows and bulls have upward curving horns. When attacked by bears or wolves, these sharp ornaments can often prove lethal to the predator.

Adult bull
6 ft TALL

Walking tracks

Bison bull study
Delta Jct., Alaska

The bison is the largest terrestrial mammal in North America.
Alaska has small free-ranging herds.

Pacific Walrus

The tusks of the Pacific walrus are actually elongated upper canine teeth, and both the males and females have them. Tusks are used for fighting (usually amongst bulls) and for climbing around on ice floes. Usually the bulls with the largest tusks can visually intimidate small bulls into moving from the choicest resting areas.

Pacific walrus (Odobenus rosmarus divergens) is an important mainstay of many Alaskan Eskimo villages. The large, migratory marine animals are utilized for food, clothing and boat coverings. A large bull weighs two tons and his huge tusks are prized by Native carvers. Mating occurs in January/February, with the calves born in April/May.

The WALRUS in Alaska

A walrus diet consists of clams and other sea-bottom invertebrates.

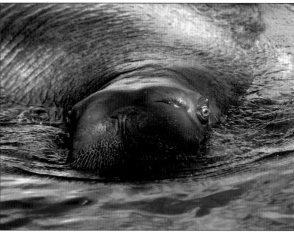

Native hunters have long respected the walrus' "protective instincts" for herd members, and many boats have been attacked in defense. Most hunting is done during spring/summer when the walrus herds are migrating north. Because of the difficult hunting conditions, it is estimated that a high percentage of shot or wounded animals are unsalvaged.

Walruses are members of a widely distributed group of marine mammals known as pinnipeds, a group which includes sea lions and seals. Walruses are most commonly found in relatively shallow water areas, close to land or ice.

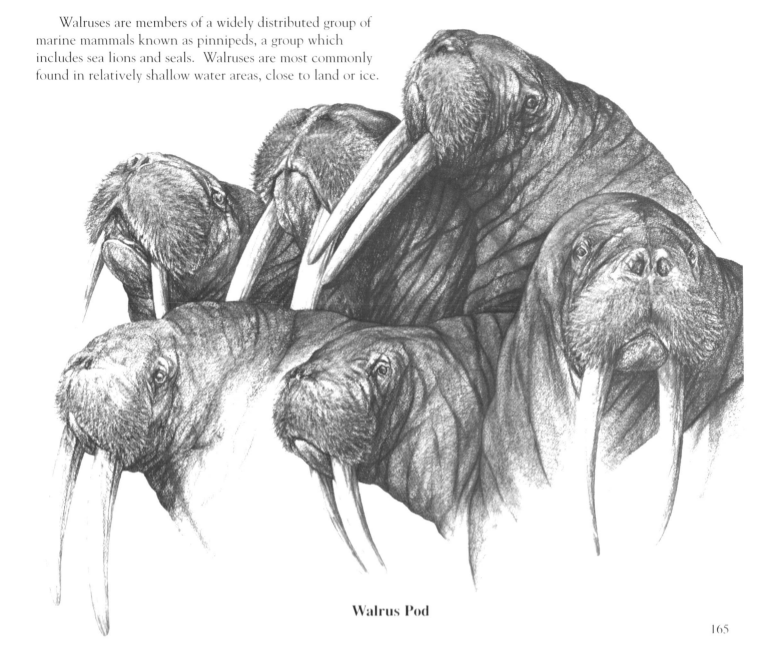

Walrus Pod

The Northern fur seal (Callorhinus ursinus) is no longer commercially hunted on the Pribilof Islands. However, subsistence hunting by Alaska's Natives is allowed and every year a certain number of seals are corralled on the beaches and harvested. The Russian and American hunters and whalers of yesteryear almost drove the Northern fur seal to extinction after their Pribilof Islands breeding and calving grounds were discovered.

Author's Journal *(June 20, '74, Pribilof Islands)*

Found five dead fox today! All were unquestionably the result of human "sport". Some unbalanced imbecile is obviously running amuck with a .22 rifle or pistol.

Spent the day amongst the rookeries; photographing puffins, murres, cormorants, auklets, gulls, kittiwakes, and nest-robbing fox.

Also, watched one fur seal bull drive a bloodied foe out of his "territory" and into anothers "territory", where the already defeated warrior was once again soundly trounced. At one time three neighboring bulls ganged up on him and unmercifully trounced him. By the time the bull finally reached the water he was covered in blood. Sharp teeth had slashed and gashed his neck, head, and shoulders. I watched him swim out into the fog shrouded sea and disappear from sight.

There were four decomposing seal carcasses at the west end of the Island. All apparent battle casualties. I fear the one bull I watched get defeated today will also be a battle casualty, as some of his cuts were serious looking (long and deep). Out at sea he becomes the helpless prey of killer whales and sharks. On shore, in his weakened condition, he will be killed by the Beachmasters (the breeding bulls) that encircle the Island; each with his own jealously-guarded harem of cows.

Today I watched three seal pups being born. The miracle of birth would be unveiled thousands of times here on this small island within the next few weeks. Thousands of birds and fur seals will soon witness the excitement of life.

A cow gave birth to a dead pup and spent the entire day guarding it from the beach-combing fox. Later at night she abandoned it.

Fur seal cows guard their pups (July / Pribilof Islands).

A gathering of fur seal cows and bulls. The dominant bull (near center) has to continuously drive away the intruding males who are located on the fringes. A sharp eye will spot the green net around the neck of one cow.

Harbor seals are common in Alaska and are normally associated with coastal waters. A mature adult is 150-200 pounds and is distinguished by its dark spots. A single pup is born in early summer.

The small, toothed, white Beluga whale feeds on fish. Recently, declining populations have deterred Native hunters from hunting them in certain locales. Whale hunting has long been a treasured custom of villagers who partially depend upon the animals for food. Marine mammals can only be hunted by Alaska's Natives.

A Beluga can remain submerged for up to 20 minutes and, if necessary, break through four inches of ice to breath. A newborn Beluga calf is gray in color and turns white when it is about six years old.

Narwhals and Belugas are restricted to the Arctic and Subarctic. Male Narwhals are distinguished by their ivory tusk; a single tooth which forms a spiral rod that may reach a few yards in length.

Author's Journal *(July 5, '75, Kenai area)*
About a dozen Beluga whales swimming around in the bay. They come in here every spring and summer to feed on the salmon that follow the Kenai River inland to spawn.

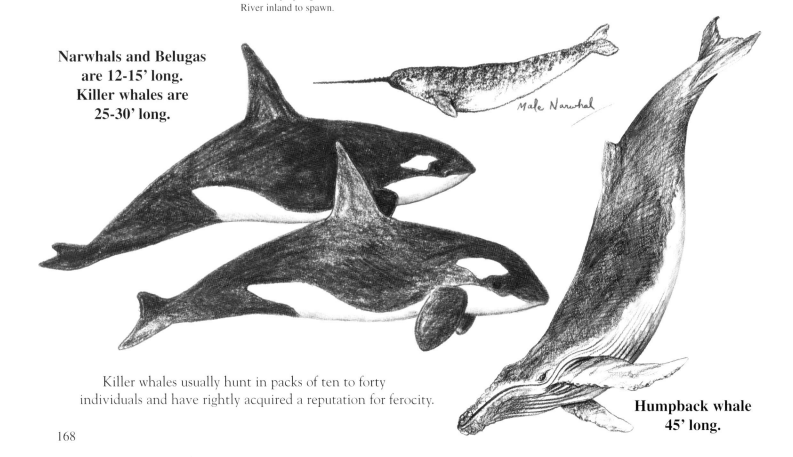

Narwhals and Belugas are 12-15' long. Killer whales are 25-30' long.

Male Narwhal

Killer whales usually hunt in packs of ten to forty individuals and have rightly acquired a reputation for ferocity.

Humpback whale 45' long.

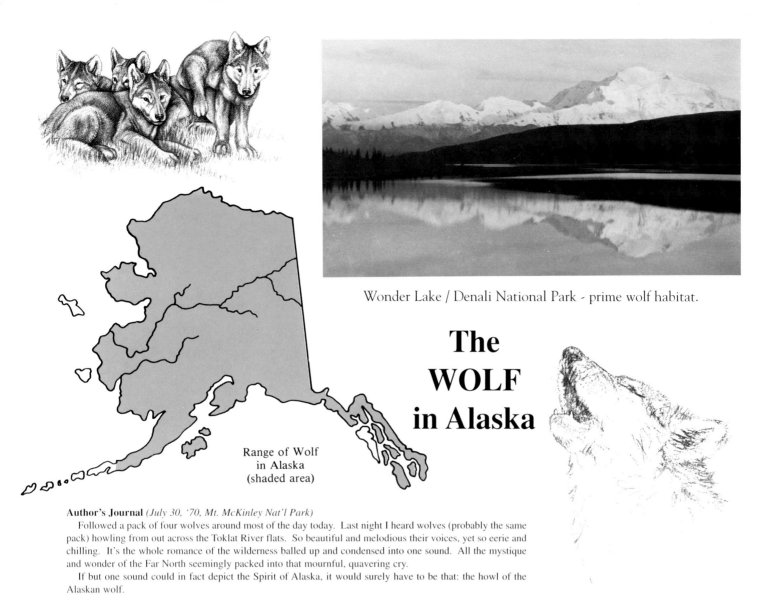

Wonder Lake / Denali National Park - prime wolf habitat.

The WOLF in Alaska

Range of Wolf
in Alaska
(shaded area)

Author's Journal *(July 30, '70, Mt. McKinley Nat'l Park)*

Followed a pack of four wolves around most of the day today. Last night I heard wolves (probably the same pack) howling from out across the Toklat River flats. So beautiful and melodious their voices, yet so eerie and chilling. It's the whole romance of the wilderness balled up and condensed into one sound. All the mystique and wonder of the Far North seemingly packed into that mournful, quavering cry.

If but one sound could in fact depict the Spirit of Alaska, it would surely have to be that: the howl of the Alaskan wolf.

Howling is thought to be a way of proclaiming territories and of maintaining contact between distant pack members.

All members of the pack help to care for the young.

Usually a wolf pack has only one breeding male and female, but the large packs may have multiple litters of pups in a single year.

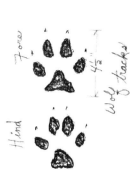

Fore

Hind

45"

Wolf tracks

The largest member of the dog family in America, the wolf (Canis lupus) occurs throughout most of Alaska. A formidable hunter, the wolves range in size from 75-100 pounds for the adult females to 80-130 pounds for the adult males. A wolf reaches full size in about a year. Pelt coloration ranges from black to white, with the darkest colored wolves roaming the southeast and the lightest colored wolves occurring in Alaska's northern arctic.

The wolf pack is a highly social and organized entity. A pack is normally made up of 5 to 20 animals, the majority of which are the parents and their offspring. Wolves tend to only roam their chosen "home range", but may overlap other packs ranges during times of prey shortages. A "home range" may range from 100 to 600 square miles. Prey is often scarce (or formidable!) and hence vast hunting areas are required to sustain the pack. Traveling 25 miles during a days hunt is not uncommon.

Wolves breed in February/March, and the "pups" are born in May/June. Litters range from 2 to 10 and are born in an underground den. By winter the pups are able to travel with the pack on its hunts. Young, inexperienced wolves often suffer high mortalities while learning how to attack Alaska's dangerous big-game animals. Hunting, trapping, and starvation are the factors affecting wolf populations.

The wolf is still usually associated with "evil" and wanton killing, but these notions are based mostly on old folk-lore and not facts. It's true that the wolf must kill to survive and does "compete" with man for their prey. They are, however, a valuable participant in the wild ecosystem of the Far North country. Were we ever to lose such a valuable predator, man would surely be the loser. Alaska has become one of the last strongholds of the wolf; may its chilling howls echo across the vast wilderness forever and ever.

Eye color will vary; note the wolves shown here.

Male

Northern wolf

**Alaskan
Wolf Study**

"Wolf Song"

Author's Journal (*July 26, '70, Mt. McKinley Nat'l Park*)
    Perhaps the reason some people have such hatred of the wolf is because he preys on the same food as man himself. Moose, sheep, caribou; these are all table fare shared by wolf and man. Is man so unwilling to share Nature's bounty? I say let the wolf live. He too deserves his niche in this puzzle we call life.

    A dominant member of a wolf pack will carry its tail high, whereas a "lesser" wolf will often tuck its tail between its legs in a submissive gesture. This social hierarchy, once established, will help maintain order within the pack.

The COYOTE in Alaska

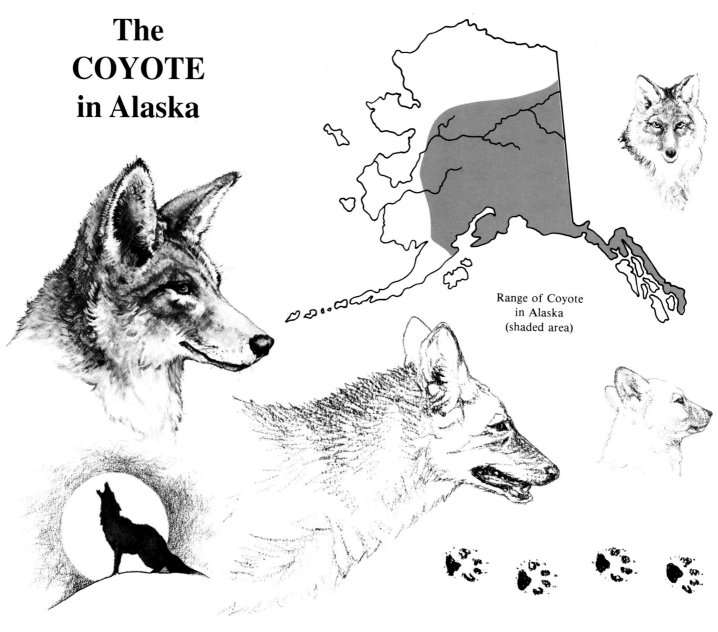

Range of Coyote
in Alaska
(shaded area)

Author's Journal *(Nov. 28, 2001)*
Returning from a road trip "outside" where I photographed Bighorns in Alberta, Montana and Wyoming. From Whitehorse (Yukon) to Palmer (Alaska) I did not see one moose or caribou, but I did see six different coyotes hunting for rodents near the highway. Every year I see more and more coyotes here in Alaska.

Coyote litters average about six pups. Coyotes are also thought to mate for life.

COYOTE TRACKS

Coyote study

Author's Journal *(May 30, '79, Anchorage area)*
Potter's marsh area. A coyote was moving off in the brush on the back side of the swamp when I "glassed" around that way. Personally, I don't like him being in here amongst all these nesting birds. A skilled fox or dog or coyote can reduce a breeding ground to shambles in a very short time–eating eggs and young and even killing adults.

The coyote (Canis latrans incolatus), a member of the dog family, is a sly, versatile and adaptable creature. Although wide ranging in Alaska, its highest populations are in the Kenai, Copper River, and Mat-Su valleys. It seems to be vacant from the farthest north areas; areas where their "big brother", the wolf, roams widely.

An adult coyote will average 25 to 30 pounds and stand 2 feet high at the shoulder. Its coat is normally gray, with areas of reddish-tan, black and white. A long, bushy tail and sharp-pointed nose and ears further distinguish the animal.

Coyotes breed in February/March and a litter is born in May/June. Similar to other predators of the North, more young are born during times of ample food supplies. Coyotes do not "pack-up" as do wolves, and the adults and young will usually disperse before winter.

The coyote is an able hunter and scavenger and seems able to flourish near cities and man. Although widely persecuted (trapped, poisoned, hunted) throughout its history, it seems able to sustain healthy populations. Also, coyotes have been known to carry rabies.

Coyote/male
Winter coat

Doug Lindstrand 2001

A coyote call is a high-pitched howl which normally ends with a series of yips. All coyotes within hearing range will join in the eerie "song".

The coyote is often seen patrolling roads looking for roadkills.

Pointed ears & nose

24" TALL

Erect, prominent ears

Black-Tipped Tail

The coyote is best described as an opportunistic eater. That is, whatever is available becomes fare, whether it is Snowshoe hares, winter-killed carrion, mice, birds or even fish and insects. They often hunt in pairs, chasing prey animals in relays which allow them to catch animals that would otherwise outrun a single coyote. Although they do, on occasion, kill larger animals such as Dall sheep, it is not a normal prey specie for them.

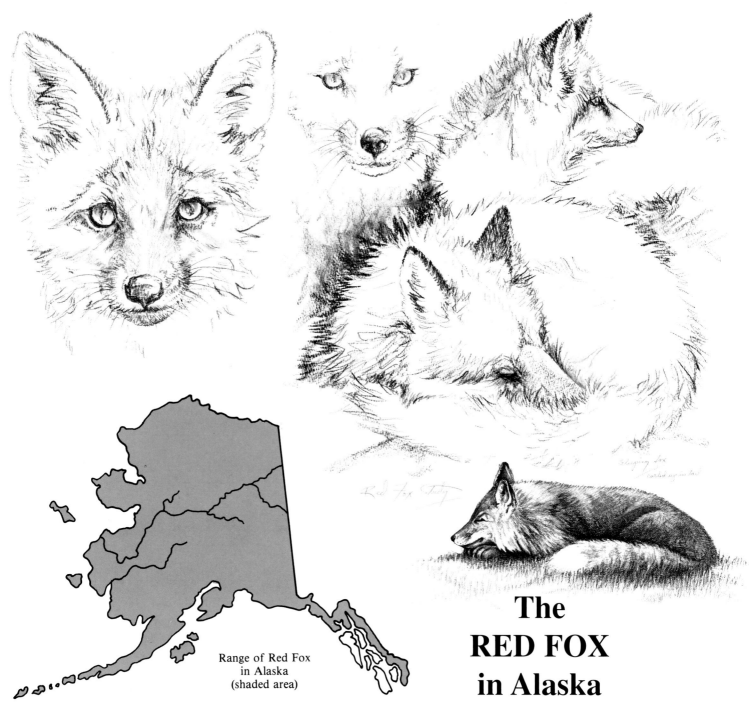

Range of Red Fox
in Alaska
(shaded area)

The
RED FOX
in Alaska

Red fox carrying Arctic ground squirrel.

The wary, sly, sharp-witted Red fox (Vulpes vulpes) is found throughout most of Alaska. It adapts well to varied environments and is omnivorous; meaning its diet consists of a wide variety of foods - from assorted vegetation to insects to birds and mammals.

Members of the dog family, the fox's coat varies from red to "silver" to black, and an adult commonly weighs 8-15 pounds. Its "black-socks" legs and white-tipped tail (15 inches long) further distinguish the animal from its wild brother, the coyote.

Although rabies, accidents and other wildlife predators take a toll on fox numbers, the biggest influence is probably human trapping. Fox fur, depending on fluctuating demands, is a big cash contributor to the subsistence lifestyle of many "bush" Alaskans.

Author's Journal *(Aug. 30, '83, Denali Nat'l Park)*
Pouring rain. Sitting in camp (under a tarp) drinking tea and roasting hotdogs.

(Aug. 31, '83, Denali Nat'l Park)
Photographed two separate fox running down the gravel road with ground squirrels in their mouths.
Both headed off into the brush and later returned empty mouthed. Delivered to den or just stashed?

Author's Journal *(Oct. 1, '70, Mt. McKinley Nat'l Park)*

His golden red coat glistening in the morning sun, the Red fox pranced gracefully along his chosen game trail, his small black-capped feet touching as lightly as a slinking cat. He pauses, listening for the faintest rustle of grass to disclose where a meal hides. Or, he creeps along flat on his stomach until his prey is within reach, then leaps out of hiding and finishes it off with a slashing of teeth.

This then is the hunting method of the Red fox I watched and followed on and off during the day. Wary, sharp-witted, and a very beautiful creature.

Also, saw a cow moose today with triplets. First set of moose triplets I've seen. Twins seem to be the most common of all moose litter sizes.

Red fox (cross phase)

A "silver" fox near Sourdough, Alaska.

Kits near den

Breeding season is February/March, with the "kits" born in April/May. Den sites are often used repeatedly and usually have several entrances. The kits grow rapidly, learn to hunt from their parents, and by the winter season are off on their own.

The ARCTIC FOX in Alaska

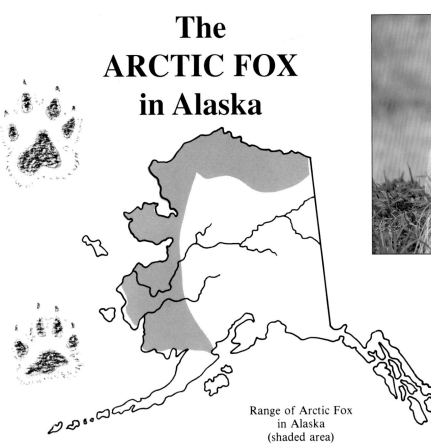

Range of Arctic Fox
in Alaska
(shaded area)

Pribilof Island fox / summer

During the summer, living is easy for foxes living near seabird nesting grounds. Prey is sometimes cached to be eaten during winter, a period of scarcity.

Winter coat

Winter

Autumn

An adult Arctic fox curls up for a short nap. Its white coat renders it temporarily conspicuous in the yet snowless landscape.

The Arctic fox (Alopex lagopus) is one of our favorite wildlife creatures. Its stocky body, short ears, long fluffy tail and "cute' face makes it seem more like a little "toy" than the able predator it truly is. An adult weighs 6-11 pounds and the specie has two color "phases": the blue and the white. The white-phase seems more common in the northernmost areas, while the blue-phase is common on the Pribilof Islands. It is common for litters to have both color phases.

Mating occurs in March/April and the "pups" are born in May/June. By their first winter the young are on their own, solitary creatures that roam widely in order to sustain life. In the far north they often follow the Polar bears and feed on left-over scraps. Seabirds and eggs are a favorite summer food of the Pribilof Island foxes. It, like the Red fox, can carry rabies.

A newborn pup leaves his litter of seven siblings to do some exploring while his mother is away hunting for lemmings and voles.

Tufted puffins (as well as their eggs and chicks) are often prey for coastal foxes.

Arctic fox in its white winter coat. In late spring its coat will turn grayish -brown to match the changing environment. In the above photo a recently awakened fox yawns.

Arctic fox have relatively small ears (unlike the more southern Red fox) which help lessen the loss of body heat during the cold winters.

The LYNX in Alaska

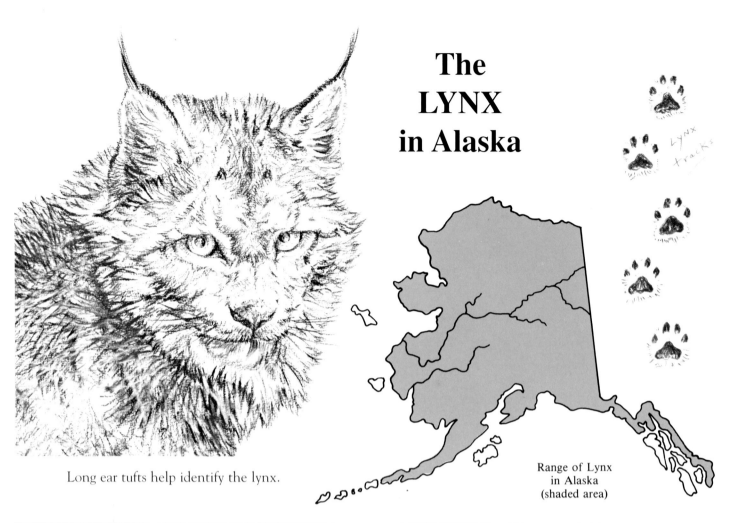

Long ear tufts help identify the lynx.

Range of Lynx
in Alaska
(shaded area)

Lynx tracks

Adult

185

The lynx (Lynx canadensis) is Alaska's only cat. They are found throughout most of Alaska and seem to run in "cycles" like their primary prey: the Snowshoe hare. Although they have a wide variety of prey, they seem significantly "connected" to the hare; and when its numbers are scarce the numbers of new lynx "kittens" decline accordingly. Long legs, "tufts" on ear-tips, and grayish-white coloration usually distinguish the lynx from its southern-cousin, the bobcat. It is normally larger also, weighing 30-40 pounds at maturity.

Alaska range / December

Snowshoe hare (summer coat)

Snowshoes are also called "varying hare", due to their coat's color change from winter white to summer brown. Their large hind feet help propel them across the snowy terrain.

A male lynx gives a curious stare, perhaps evaluating whether his newly acquired rodent "kill" is in jeopardy.

The large broad paws of the lynx helps make it one of the few predators that can substantially prey on the Snowshoe hare during the snowy winters.

Lynx tracks

Lynx / October 2000
Tok, Alaska

Lynx kittens (October)

Kittens are normally born in May/June, often in a brush deadfall. Usually the family will remain together until the adults again mate. The year's young, if prey is scarce, often will not survive their first winter. Also, being curious creatures, they are often more easily trapped than their older and wiser parents. Life expectancy is usually 10-15 years in the wild.

The
WOLVERINE
in Alaska

The wolverine (Gulo gulo) is a fierce wilderness wanderer and exists throughout much of Alaska. Often nicknamed "skunk bear" because of its habit of fouling its prey with its repugnant scent, it is often a scourge of a wilderness trapper whose trapped quarry often becomes food to the wolverine and thus a destroyed fur. Its keen sense of smell and clever antics make it difficult to trap, but the fur of those trapped is extremely valuable for parka hood trim, as the guard hairs of its fur resist frost build-up.

A member of the weasel family, an adult may have a body length of about 42 inches and weigh up to 35 pounds. Normally they can live 10-15 years in the wilderness. "Kits" are born usually around March and are on their own by the following winter. Their overlapping hunting ranges often cover over a hundred square miles.

Range of Wolverine
in Alaska
(shaded area)

Wolverine
tracks

A formidable foe, the vicious wolverine has been known to drive grizzly bears from a kill. Also, under certain snow conditions, they are easily capable of killing big game animals.

The wolverine, like most carnivores, has large teeth and powerful jaws for capturing and eating prey. Snowshoe hares and carrion are its principal food, but grouse, ptarmigan and small mammals also supplement their diet.

Wolverines do not hibernate. In winter, the wolverine's coat becomes very thick and the soles of their feet are covered with stiff hair to facilitate walking in snow.

Author's Journal *(Dec. 19, '71, Mankomen lake)*
Saw one of nature's "rarest children" today. This morning I watched a wolverine walk up the frozen creek outside my cabin. Too "cool" for words!

A yawning wolverine shows his deadly teeth.

The Wolverine is nicknamed "skunk bear."

Rear Paw

TRACKS

Solitary, hunts by stealth.
In Alaska the wolverine is very destructive
to trappers, as it will eat the trapped animals.

SMALL MAMMALS

The Red squirrel (Tamiasciurus hudsonicus) is found throughout much of Alaska. A small, rusty and white colored animal, it is one of nature's seemingly "busiest" creatures, constantly eating or stashing foods for the long winter season. Spruce cones, berries, seeds and mushrooms make up most of their diet. Owls and marten are their main predators.

The Northern Flying squirrel (Glaucomys subrinus) is a small, nocturnal squirrel that glides from tree to tree by spreading their legs and stretching their flight skin. Their tail acts as a rudder. Normally has only one litter (2-5 young) per year.

The Collared pika (Ochotona collaris) is related to rabbits and is often nicknamed "rock bunny". Small (6 ounces) and wary, the pika lives in colonies in mountainous, rocky terrain. Females bear two litters during the summer. Pikas do not hibernate like ground squirrels, but live off its "haystacks": piles of vegetation that is harvested and stored during the growing season. Haystacks can often reach 2-3 feet high by autumn and the sun-dried food usually sustains them until spring. Fox and weasels are major predators.

Alaska has a varied and substantial population of other small mammals that often make up a large percentage of the prey of predators. They feed fox, lynx, ravens, owls, eagles, weasels and, at times, each other (as is the case with voles and shrews). Widespread throughout the state, they normally have several litters yearly. Life expectancy is only about one year.

There are also 5 species of bats living in Alaska, all nocturnal. Unique and able hunters, the winged mammals are thought to "hibernate" through much of the winter. They normally give birth in May and life expectancy can be 20 years. Although seldom seen by humans, the bats provide us with a valuable service, eating mosquitoes in huge numbers. The big Brown bat, Alaska's largest, weighs 1/2 ounce.

Alaska's tiny Red squirrel does not hibernate, but will sometimes hole-up in nests or hollow trees during the coldest weather.

Northern Flying squirrel

Red squirrel

Author's Journal *(Feb. 1, '82, Susitna valley)*
Red squirrels will defend their few acre territories from other squirrels. During winter they depend upon their stored caches of spruce cones for survival.

Squirrel Tracks

DEER MOUSE BROWN COAT

Beaver

Mount McKinley towers above a lodge in Denali National Park. Muskrats and beavers both build lodges within which they raise their young and find safety from predators.

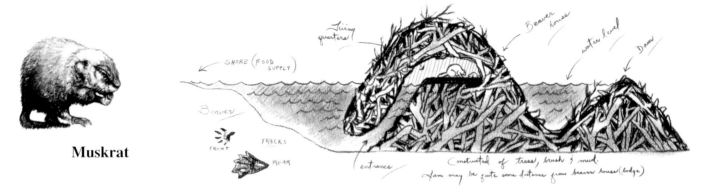

Muskrat

The beaver has two pair of gnawing teeth, one pair in the upper jaw and the other in the lower. These large front teeth enables the industrious rodent to fell large trees and hence provide itself with food and building supplies for its dams and house. No other creature has so altered Alaska's landscape.

Beavers are Alaska's largest rodent and can weigh up to sixty pounds. Willow leaves and bark are its primary food.

Few animals in the world can match the Sea otter for intelligence and adaptability. Although once nearly wiped-out by fur hunters in the 18th century, the graceful, playful, bewhiskered little creatures have rebounded in numbers and now are commonly seen in certain areas along Alaska's coastlines.

An adult can weigh over 80 pounds and measure four feet long. Their heads and throats are normally off-white while the remainder of their bodies are a darkish brown.

Hunderds of otters are estimated to have died during the devastating 1989 oil spill near Valdez, Alaska.

Sea otters

Wood frogs survive the long, Alaska winters by freezing themselves solid. Upon thawing-out, the small frogs mate and lay eggs.

Land otter

Author's Journal *(Oct. 19, '80, Beaver Lakes)*
    3 land otters were sitting on my dock this morning. First time I've seen them. Either they live up the creek or else they're on a cross country trek looking for a new home. Two adults and one young.
    A lot of ducks here at the lake. Bunching up for flight south.

The HARE in Alaska

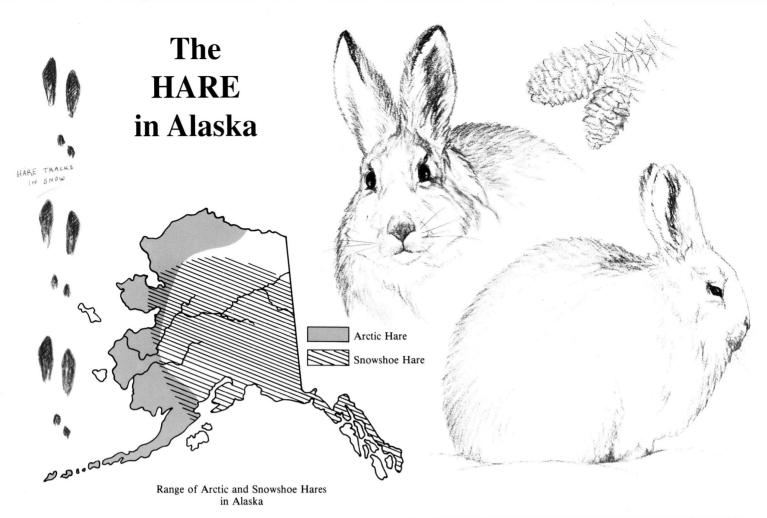

HARE TRACKS IN SNOW

Arctic Hare

Snowshoe Hare

Range of Arctic and Snowshoe Hares
in Alaska

Snowshoe hare (winter coat)

198

Lynx

Snowshoe hare (October)

Two species of hares are found in Alaska: the Varying hare (or snowshoe) and the Arctic hare. Both turn white in winter, and the larger (up to 12 pounds) Arctic hare is not as widely dispersed as the 4 pound "snowshoe".

The more common Varying hare tends to run in population "cycles". It has numerous litters per year and is an important food source of many Alaskan predators (such as lynx, fox, and wolverines) whose own population often correlate accordingly.

Care should always be taken when cleaning or cooking harvested hares, as tularemia may be present.

Red fox (summer)

Wolverine

Marten

Collared pika

Martens exist in Alaska from the southeast all the way north to where the trees end and the arctic tundra begins. Its rich coat varies from brown to yellowish, with an orangish throat and chest. An adult weighs about 3 pounds and is about 2 feet long. Voles, mice, squirrels, eggs and berries are its primary diet. Except for the mating season, marten are solitary creatures.

Marten

Author's Journal *(July 21, '78, Healy, Alaska)*
Pikas are very social and vocal, and the colony scatters at the slightest disturbance. <u>Very</u> hard to photograph due to their small size and jitteryness.

VOLE
(MEADOW VOLE, SINGING VOLE
TUNDRA VOLE, CHESTNUT-CHEEKED VOLE)

WHEN FOOD IS ABUNDANT A FEMALE CAN
PRODUCE UP TO 30 YOUNG PER YEAR.

Pika

Pikas reside in rock slides adjacent to alpine meadows. They do not hibernate, but instead spend the winters eating the vegetation that they have spent the previous summer gathering and stacking into "haystacks" beneath the rocks.

Marten

201

Author's Journal *(Aug. 20, '01, Whittier)*
    Spent the day with a colony of marmots near Whittier. Sunny and 70°. They feed almost entirely on grasses and other plants and since I saw various adults carry mouthfuls of grass into their burrows, I assume they use them to line their hibernation nests. Also, everytime two marmots would meet they would engage in a "wrestling match" ritual.

    The Hoary marmot is one of the three species of marmots that reside in Alaska. A mature adult can weigh over 10 pounds and reach 24" in length. True hibernators, they emerge from their winter quarters in April/May.

    Hoary marmots make their homes at the bases of active talus slopes, where the rocks provide shelter and lookout perches. When predators such as wolves, fox, or eagles are spotted, the lookout marmot alarms the colony with a loud, shrill whistle. The pelt colors of marmots help them blend in with the rusty-brown rocky terrain they inhabit.

Golden eagle

The Arctic ground squirrel is a very important prey animal in Alaska. Weighing about a pound, this reddish-gray creature is normally plentiful and is a favorite of bears, eagles, owls and fox.

Arctic ground squirrel

Arctic ground squirrel

Porcupine

Porcupines spend much of their lives perched up in trees eating. During spring and summer they feast on buds and young leaves. The inner bark of trees make up its winter diet. Although mainly nocturnal, they often are seen during the day moving to a new tree.

One enduring animal myth is that the porcupine shoots its quills at its enemies. The "porky" lashes out with its tail but does not "shoot" quills. If the enemy is within range of the lashed tail, the barbed quills will be embedded in it. Many predators, large and small, have died after receiving a mouthful or pawful of quills, rendering it unable to hunt or feed.

The porcupine is second in size only to the beaver amongst rodents in Alaska. About 2 feet long, an adult can weigh over 20 pounds.

When threatened, a porcupine tries to keep its back facing the attacker and flips its quilled tail when approached.

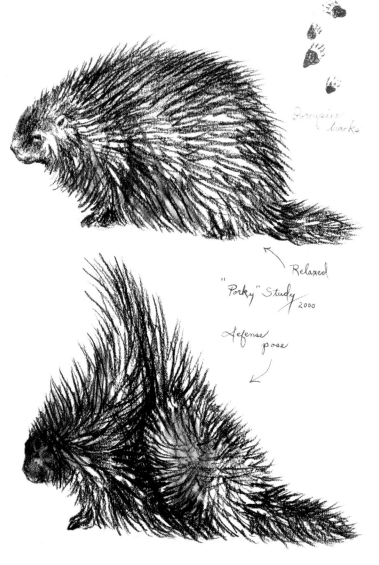

Porcupine tracks

Relaxed

"Porky" Study 2000

Defense pose

During the summer months, Alaska's roads are crowded with tourists and residents. Unfortunately, newborn and adult wildlife often are casualties. Here an orphaned baby porcupine is hand-fed to adulthood.

Grizzly cubs at play

<u>COMMENTARY</u>

Alaska, the Great Land. Alaska is one of the world's great wildlife sanctuaries and one of the world's most hazardous and harshest environments. A land of self-sufficient and independent people of an adventurous and curious nature. A land awesomely rich in resources and beauty. A fragile land as yet untamed and wild.

We who live here have seen the "changes" that have beset Alaska in recent years. Some refer to it as "progress"; others call it "plunder". We all walk in different moccasins and so each of our outlooks is different. Some of us, for example, live to watch grizzlies roam the mountain meadows; others live to kill grizzlies at every encounter with a passion born both of fear and hatred. And, since all of us Alaskans and visitors live side by side, we must adopt some sort of common and sensible path. Therefore, if we all reach into our hearts and do what we truly know is both moral and correct, we will have made a big step towards preserving Alaska's beauty and greatness and of helping this unique and bountiful land retain its rightful claim as "America's Jewel".

Let us all strive to help keep Alaska beautiful. To not just "take" but to also "preserve". Explore and enjoy, but tread lightly. Be a friend to "wild Alaska".